THE COUNTERCULTURE MOVEMENT OF THE 1960s

AMERICAN
SOCIAL
MOVEMENTS

THE
COUNTERCULTURE
MOVEMENT
OF THE 1960s

William S. McConnell, *Book Editor*

Bruce Glassman, *Vice President*
Bonnie Szumski, *Publisher*
Helen Cothran, *Managing Editor*

**GREENHAVEN
PRESS®**

THOMSON
™
GALE

San Diego • Detroit • New York • San Francisco • Cleveland
New Haven, Conn. • Waterville, Maine • London • Munich

For more information, contact
Greenhaven Press
27500 Drake Rd.
Farmington Hills, MI 48331-3535
Or you can visit our Internet site at http://www.gale.com

Cover credit: © Bettmann/CORBIS
Library of Congress, 17, 27, 85, 96, 111, 118
National Archives, 14, 159

LIBRARY OF CONGRESS CATALOGING-IN-PUBLICATION DATA

Counterculture movement of the 1960s / William S. McConnell, book editor.
     p. cm. — (American social movements)
     Includes bibliographical references and index.
     ISBN 0-7377-1819-6 (lib. : alk. paper)
     1. United States—Social conditions—1960–1980. 2. Counterculture—United States—History—20th century. 3. Protest movements—United States—History—20th century. 4. United States—History—1961–1969. 5. United States—Intellectual life—20th century. 6. Nineteen sixties. I. McConnell, William S. II. Series.
     HN59.C67 2004
     306'.0973—dc22   2003061114

CONTENTS

such as wealth to establish a new and better society reflecting youthful ideals.

Chapter 3 • BLACK POWER AND CIVIL RIGHTS IN THE MID-1960s

Chapter 4 • THE SEXUAL REVOLUTION OF THE LATE 1960s

Chapter 5 • VIOLENCE AND THE ANTIWAR MOVEMENT OF THE LATE 1960s

FOREWORD

Historians Gary T. Marx and Douglas McAdam define a social movement as "organized efforts to promote or resist change in society that rely, at least in part, on noninstitutionalized forms of political action." Examining American social movements broadens and vitalizes the study of history by allowing students to observe the efforts of ordinary individuals and groups to oppose the established values of their era, often in unconventional ways. The civil rights movement of the twentieth century, for example, began as an effort to challenge legalized racial segregation and garner social and political rights for African Americans. Several grassroots organizations—groups of ordinary citizens committed to social activism—came together to organize boycotts, sit-ins, voter registration drives, and demonstrations to counteract racial discrimination. Initially, the movement faced massive opposition from white citizens, who had long been accustomed to the social standards that required the separation of the races in almost all areas of life. But the movement's consistent use of an innovative form of protest—nonviolent direct action—eventually aroused the public conscience, which in turn paved the way for major legislative victories such as the Civil Rights Act of 1964 and the Voting Rights Act of 1965. Examining the civil rights movement reveals how ordinary people can use nonstandard political strategies to change society.

Investigating the style, tactics, personalities, and ideologies of American social movements also encourages students to learn about aspects of history and culture that may receive scant attention in textbooks. As scholar Eric Foner notes, American history "has been constructed not only in congressional debates and political treatises, but also on plantations and picket lines, in parlors and bedrooms. Frederick Douglass, Eugene V. Debs, and Margaret Sanger . . . are its architects as well as Thomas Jefferson and Abraham Lincoln." While not all

American social movements garner popular support or lead to epoch-changing legislation, they each offer their own unique insight into a young democracy's political dialogue.

Each book in Greenhaven's American Social Movements series allows readers to follow the general progression of a particular social movement—examining its historical roots and beginnings in earlier chapters and relatively recent and contemporary information (or even the movement's demise) in later chapters. With the incorporation of both primary and secondary sources, as well as writings by both supporters and critics of the movement, each anthology provides an engaging panoramic view of its subject. Selections include a variety of readings, such as book excerpts, newspaper articles, speeches, manifestos, literary essays, interviews, and personal narratives. The editors of each volume aim to include the voices of movement leaders and participants as well as the opinions of historians, social analysts, and individuals who have been affected by the movement. This comprehensive approach gives students the opportunity to view these movements both as participants have experienced them and as historians and critics have interpreted them.

Every volume in the American Social Movements series includes an introductory essay that presents a broad historical overview of the movement in question. The annotated table of contents and comprehensive index help readers quickly locate material of interest. Each selection is preceded by an introductory paragraph that summarizes the article's content and provides historical context when necessary. Several other research aids are also present, including brief excerpts of supplementary material, a chronology of major events pertaining to the movement, and an accessible bibliography.

The Greenhaven Press American Social Movements series offers readers an informative introduction to some of the most fascinating groups and ideas in American history. The contents of each anthology provide a valuable resource for general readers as well as for enthusiasts of American political science, history, and culture.

INTRODUCTION

The term *counterculture* is used to characterize the various philosophies, movements, and activist groups that sought to change America's political and cultural landscape during the 1960s. The original impetus for change came from students who were increasingly discontent with the moral and social norms governing the lives of their parents' generation. These mainly white, middle-class university students began to question the goals set forth for them, including attaining an advanced degree, procuring steady, well-paid employment, and pursuing the American dream of a house and family in the suburbs. They also began to challenge the conservative policies of state and federal government. Specifically, they became aware of racial injustice in the American South, and they questioned what they perceived as the complacency of their elders and the status quo. Initially, student radicals involved themselves in the burgeoning civil rights movement, helping to bring national media attention to the African American struggle. As these students voiced their opinions in the media and participated in protest movements on the streets of major cities, the student activist movement was born. The New Left, as these students came to call themselves, contributed to victories for the civil rights movement and helped to create more opportunities for women in the workplace. It also protested U.S. participation in the Vietnam War.

THE BIRTH OF NEW LEFT RADICALISM

Political involvement at the community level had been stressed since the beginning of the 1960s, when President John F. Kennedy stated in his inaugural address on January 20, 1961, "Ask not what your country can do for you, ask what you can do for your country. . . . Ask not what America will do for you, but what together we can do for the freedom of man."[1] Kennedy's statement seemed to be a new mandate for Americans, including students, to contribute to making positive changes in the nation.

Many student activists had been exposed to the inherent possibilities of change that political action offered while participating in the civil rights struggle in the late 1950s and early 1960s. However, these early activists often felt frustrated by the limitations placed on them by segregationists in state and local government that prevented them from making substantial changes. In response, students decided to form their own national activism organization, Students for a Democratic Society (SDS). In June 1962 student activist and SDS cofounder Tom Hayden met with several other student activists in Port Huron, Michigan, to outline what they believed should be the direction of this new, national, student-led protest organization. This core group decided that SDS should work within local communities to secure social reform and welfare programs for underrepresented members of society, including students, African Americans, women, and the poor.

At this meeting, Tom Hayden wrote the Port Huron Statement, which established the SDS concept of participatory democracy. Participatory democracy required political action to occur at every level of society so that all members of a community received representation through their elected officials and access to social welfare programs. SDS called for this new type of community action as a response to what student radicals viewed as the federal government's growing disinterest in the needs of local communities. From the perspective of SDS, Congress was so focused on its attempts to quell the global spread of communism that it was failing to address the nation's ailing network of social programs. As Congress and the president committed themselves to fighting communism, money was shifted to military budgets instead of into domestic social programs. In the view of SDS, by not addressing important social issues such as homelessness, poverty, low-income housing, employment, and health care, the federal government had failed to make the needs of the American people a priority. Many student activists felt it was their duty to take action to get the government to address these needs.

THE EMERGENCE OF THE HIPPIE CULTURE

From 1963 to 1965, New Left students became involved in two related movements: the free speech movement (which originated at the University of California at Berkeley as students protested to win the right to conduct political action on university campuses) and the burgeoning anti–Vietnam War movement. Students held rallies, marches, and sit-ins to protest U.S. policy in Vietnam. These demonstrations were broadcast into American homes via television. On college campuses, teach-ins (professor- and student-led seminars that educated activists on the impact of the Vietnam War) and other protest activities took place frequently. America's young people increasingly spoke out against government entities representing the system they sought to challenge. As if to accentuate the clash in values between older and younger Americans, youthful Americans adopted changes in their appearance. Many grew long hair and wore nonconventional clothing. They also listened to rock music, experimented with drugs, and engaged in casual sex. Furthermore, student activists and other young Americans spurned the pursuit of material gain. Owning a home, pursuing a career, and raising a family no longer appeared to be worthwhile goals. Instead, they experimented with various forms of communal living with the ideal of sharing possessions and helping others. These counterculturalists became known as hippies. Sociologist and activist Fred Davis characterized hippies as

> originating mainly in the middle-class [and] nurtured at the boards of consumer abundance. Spared their parents' vivid memories of economic depression and material want, however, they now declare unshamefacedly that the very quest for the good things in life and all that this entails—the latest model, the third car, the monthly credit payments, the right house in the right neighborhood—are a "bad bag."[2]

This shift in social values reflected the idealism set forth by

SDS in 1962 in the Port Huron Statement.

Throughout the 1960s, thousands of hippie youths migrated to San Francisco, claiming the city as a mecca for the new hippie culture. Between 1963 and 1968, San Francisco's Haight-Ashbury neighborhood was transformed from a depressed

A protester burns a draft card during an antiwar rally. During the 1960s hippies often participated in demonstrations against the Vietnam War.

commercial district into a haven for artists, writers, and activists. Haight-Ashbury consisted of a nine-block area beginning at Haight Street and extending west toward Golden Gate Park. People were drawn to the area because of its reputation for moral tolerance. Musicians, runaways, and social dropouts alike flocked to this area to experiment with drugs, especially LSD. Davis describes the counterculture's fascination with illicit substances: "Drugs impart to the present—or so it is alleged by the hippie psychedelic religionists—an aura of aliveness, a sense of union with fellow man and nature which can be apprehended only after the deepest reflection of and self-knowledge induced by protracted experience."[3] For many in the Haight-Ashbury hippie culture, using LSD was a rite of passage.

Initially, Haight-Ashbury thrived and many businesses opened to cater to the new subculture. By 1966 an estimated fifteen thousand hippies lived in the area. The number of homeless people rose drastically, and many people found it difficult to find employment. One activist group, the Diggers, provided for the needs of many of these destitute individuals through their free store and soup kitchen operations. However, by the end of the summer of 1968, the ever-increasing number of runaways and hippies seeking to visit the mecca overburdened the city. Without enough jobs, residences, or resources to cater to the thousands of people who had moved into the area, Haight-Ashbury lost its appeal and eventually returned to its former status as a depressed commercial district.

THE STRUGGLE FOR CIVIL RIGHTS AND THE RISE OF BLACK POWER

In the 1960s the "separate but equal" policy that supposedly ensured that blacks and whites would have separate but equal access to voting booths, education, and public services had in fact left African American facilities underfunded and underdeveloped. The civil rights movement struggled to end such discrimination.

The best-known civil rights leader of the 1960s was Martin Luther King Jr. King began his fight against Jim Crow laws and other obstacles to equality in 1955 when he helped organize the Montgomery, Alabama, bus boycott. The protest he led resulted in a 1956 Supreme Court ruling that the Montgomery segregation law was illegal. In 1957 King established his own activist group called the Southern Christian Leadership Conference (SCLC). The SCLC's purpose was to encourage civil rights activists to pressure Congress to pass civil rights legislation. The SCLC also coordinated its efforts with those of other groups, such as the Student Nonviolent Coordinating Committee (SNCC), which also worked to end discrimination against African Americans.

King and other members of SCLC and SNCC coordinated the 1963 March on Washington, one of the largest protest demonstrations in American history, involving more than 250,000 participants in the nation's capital. There he delivered his now famous "I Have a Dream" speech. After the passage of the 1964 Civil Rights Act (which guaranteed equal access to all public facilities for all minority groups by removing the "separate but equal" policy), King remained active in other human rights causes, such as the fight against poverty and the war in Vietnam, until his assassination in 1968.

In the early 1960s the National Association for the Advancement of Colored People (NAACP) and SNCC led voter registration drives in Alabama, Georgia, and Mississippi. The voter registration drives were a strategy designed to combat discriminatory practices at voting booths. Many southern states had policies in place that allowed local governments to assess a poll tax before an election, a tax that most poor blacks could not afford to pay. Those unable to pay the tax forfeited their right to vote in that particular election. Although the tax could be assessed on white voters, this policy was never enforced in the white community.

Literacy tests were also used to discriminate against black voters. The purpose of the literacy test was to show that an individual could read the ballot well enough to make informed choices. Both white and black voters had to pass the test in order to register to vote. However, local communities administered literacy exams that were far above the skill level of poor and undereducated black voter applicants while giving easier tests to white voter applicants. Many African Americans were thus prevented from having a powerful voice in legislative decisions. For example, fewer than eight thousand blacks were registered to vote in Mississippi because of discriminatory practices.

The NAACP's voter registration efforts in Mississippi were spearheaded by a young and optimistic African American named Medgar Evers. According to historian Kate Tuttle, "Evers was outspoken, and his demands were radical for his rigidly segregated state."[4] Evers advanced his belief in the unhindered right to vote by working door-to-door to register

On August 28, 1963, more than 250,000 people from across the nation gathered for the March on Washington.

black voters. With fellow activist Aaron Henry, Evers engineered the Freedom Vote Campaign, which was designed to register black voters by teaching African Americans how to pass the literacy tests. Evers held community education meetings to tutor African Americans in essential reading skills as well as to organize protests against the practice of literacy testing as a prerequisite to voting. Unfortunately, his work was ended when a white supremacist named Byron de la Beckwith shot Evers in the back as he returned home from work on June 12, 1963.

Although Evers did not live to see the passage of key legislation by Congress in 1964 and 1965 ensuring access to the ballot, his legacy lives on in the South. After his murder, the NAACP continued to work against the segregationist policies of the South. Jackson, Mississippi, and other southern cities benefited greatly from his work with the NAACP. According to Doris P. Smith, an African American activist and member of the Jackson city council, "Medgar would be impressed at how broad-minded and enlightened the white leadership has become. The needs of the black community are now being taken seriously, and blacks are beginning to understand the significance of representing their needs seriously and competently themselves."[5]

THE STUDENT NONVIOLENT COORDINATING COMMITTEE

On February 1, 1960, in Greensboro, North Carolina, four African American college students sat down at a lunch counter at an all-white restaurant at Woolworth's. The next day, thirty students joined the sit-in. By the end of the week, sixty black students were sitting in all of the spaces reserved for whites. The store owner became frustrated with the protesters and temporarily closed the lunch counter in support of his "whites only" policy, but by then the local media had heavily covered the students' actions. The concept of sit-ins quickly spread to other communities in North Carolina and then to the surrounding states. By April sit-ins were occurring in every southern state and involved more than fifty thousand activists. SNCC was founded on the campus of Shaw University in Raleigh, North Carolina, to coordinate these sit-ins. Nonviolent tactics became the cornerstone of SNCC political strategy for the next six years and would be a successful tool for achieving fairness at the polls and civil rights. SNCC members held to their policy of nonviolent protests even when faced with brutal violence from the opposition. Because their protests were often televised, this tactic won SNCC much public sympathy.

One of SNCC's biggest successes was its organization of the Freedom Rides movement in 1961 to challenge segregation on interstate buses and in bus terminals. Although the Supreme Court had ruled in *Boynton v. Virginia* in 1960 that segregation in interstate travel was illegal, federal authorities were still enforcing discriminatory policies.

African American passengers were still required to give up seats to white patrons on interstate bus lines and to wait in segregated passenger waiting rooms. On the Freedom Rides, black students tested the ruling by sitting at the front of the bus and refusing to move and by using other public facilities reserved for whites. Riding from Washington, D.C., to Montgomery, Alabama, the Freedom Riders faced violent opposition from segregationists in the Deep South. According to SNCC historian John Winters,

> At the Greyhound bus station in Rock Hill, South Carolina, the group encountered violence. A mob of twenty attacked the group, and [SNCC chairman] John Lewis was the first to be hit as he approached the white [passenger] waiting room. Police eventually interfered and the group was allowed access to the white waiting room. The journey continued to Georgia. After leaving Atlanta, the Greyhound bus was stopped as it entered Alabama. A mob surrounded the bus, the tires were slashed, and the bus was set on fire. The bus was burned to the ground.[6]

On May 29, twenty-five days after the start of the Freedom Rides, the Kennedy administration announced that it had di-

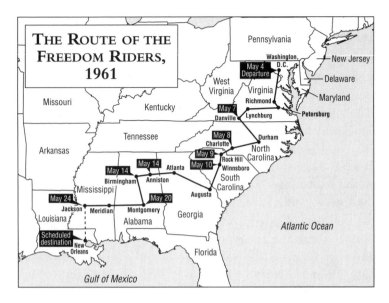

THE ROUTE OF THE FREEDOM RIDERS, 1961

Pennsylvania

West Virginia

Virginia

Missouri

Kentucky

New Jersey

Delaware

Maryland

Washington, D.C.

May 4 Departure

Richmond

Petersburg

May 7

Danville

Lynchburg

Tennessee

May 8

Charlotte

Durham

North Carolina

Arkansas

May 9

Rock Hill

May 14

May 14

Atlanta

May 10

Winnsboro

South Carolina

Birmingham

Anniston

Mississippi

May 24

May 20

Augusta

Jackson

Meridian

Montgomery

Georgia

Louisiana

Alabama

Scheduled destination

New Orleans

Florida

Atlantic Ocean

Gulf of Mexico

rected the Interstate Commerce Commission to ban segregation in all facilities under its jurisdiction. The legacy of the Rides was that those involved in the campaign learned that provoking white violence through nonviolent confrontations could attract national attention and force federal action.

SNCC's primary role as a nonviolent advocate for civil rights ended in 1966 when John Lewis stepped down as SNCC chairman. He was replaced by Stokely Carmichael. Carmichael advocated a strategy of direct confrontation. As a participant in several successful nonviolent campaigns, Carmichael was frustrated and angered by the amount of violence used against his fellow protesters. In 1963 he began to develop his own philosophy, which he called Black Power. This philosophy advocated that African Americans take control of their own communities and end their reliance upon white activists. Carmichael removed all white personnel from positions of authority within SNCC and replaced them with African Americans. He also advocated that protesters end their reliance on nonviolent strategies. In 1966, under Carmichael's direction, SNCC abandoned its policy of nonviolent protest and moved forward with a strategy of direct confrontation. His new philosophy established the Black Power movement. Carmichael resigned from his position with the SNCC in 1967 due to his increased involvement with the Black Panther Party.

THE BLACK PANTHER PARTY

The Black Panther Party was established in Oakland, California, by Huey Newton and Bobby Seale in October 1966. Newton and Seale organized this militant activist group in order to rally the black neighborhoods of Oakland in response to what they perceived as the physical brutality of police officers. Newton and Seale also educated people in the local neighborhoods of Oakland about the issues of poverty and violence in the black community, focusing on the need for better public schools and affordable housing. They also demanded full-time employment for black workers and exemption of black men from military service.

Both Newton and Seale were influenced by the militant Muslim leader Malcolm X, whose early speeches and rhetoric called on the black community to take by force what it could not get through nonviolence, a philosophy he made famous in the phrase "the ballot or the bullet." Many Muslim groups in Harlem, Baltimore, and other major areas had established community patrols to protect local black residents. Following this model of community protection, the Black Panthers also established patrols in Oakland in order to monitor police activities and protect the residents from police brutality. When confronted with police violence, the Black Panthers fought back, becoming famous in the media for their use of violence as a protest strategy. Many African American activists, frustrated with the nonviolent teachings of civil rights leader Martin Luther King Jr., became enthralled with this new form of activism that advocated physical confrontation. The militancy of the Black Panther Party quickly attracted the support of many black residents in Oakland.

The rise of such a popular militant philosophy was given special scrutiny by the federal government. Black Power advocates, militant Muslims, and some members of the Black Panther Party soon came under federal investigation for inciting violence and riots, as well as for condoning a violent response to police and National Guard units within local communities.

One individual who came under federal scrutiny was the newly elected SNCC chairman H. Rap Brown, who took the position in 1967 after Stokely Carmichael stepped down. A militant activist like Carmichael, Brown taught young, urban black males throughout the United States to take back their communities by establishing businesses that would help build a community's economic base and voting as a bloc on specific issues that affected black citizens. He also told these young men that integration and nonviolent protest were ineffective areas of focus for the black community. He advocated violence to achieve the goals of the Black Panther Party.

Brown realized early on that he would become a target of federal prosecution. As he states in his memoir of that period, *Die Nigger, Die!*,

> It was obvious when I became chairman [of SNCC] that I was in for trouble. For a year, "The Man" [white authority] had let [Stokely] Carmichael travel the country talking about Black Power and the man realized he had made a serious mistake. He realized too late that black people, like the Vietnamese, were escalating a war of liberation.[7]

In 1970 Brown went into hiding in order to avoid charges of inciting a riot in Cambridge, Maryland. In 1971 he was wounded and captured during a shoot-out with New York City police while holding up a bar. He spent fifteen years in prison for armed robbery, during which time he converted to Islam and changed his name to Imam Jamil Al-Amin. In the years after prison, he worked with local activist groups to clean up drugs and prostitution within his community. However, in 2002 he was found guilty of the March 16, 2001, murder of a Fulton County, Alabama, sheriff's deputy, who was killed while trying to deliver Al-Amin an arrest warrant for impersonating a police officer and receiving stolen goods. He is now serving a life sentence.

In 1967 Huey Newton was arrested for killing an Oakland police officer during a dispute. The cause of the killing was unclear. In order to garner support for their party's founder, Black Panther Party members created a media frenzy in an effort to disrupt the investigation. In September 1968, after a heavily publicized trial, Newton was convicted of manslaughter, but the conviction was later overturned due to prosecutorial mistakes.

Throughout the late 1960s, Black Panther Party members continued to face legal trouble. One of the most notable examples occurred in August 1968, when Bobby Seale was indicted in a Chicago federal court for conspiracy to incite a riot across state lines. Seale was indicted with seven other defendants because of their protest activities during the 1968 National Democratic Convention in Chicago. During the trial, Bobby Seale was not allowed to call witnesses in his defense and at one point was ordered bound and gagged by the trial judge, Julius Hoffman. The charges were eventually dropped in 1970. The impact of the imprisonment of important Black Panther members achieved the effect desired by the government: the removal of leadership within the Black Panther Party in order to stop the militarization of urban blacks in local communities.

THE ANTIWAR MOVEMENT

As early as 1950 the United States became involved in Vietnam. At this time, South Vietnam was under the control of the French. President Harry S. Truman established a military presence in South Vietnam to assist the French in their occupation. In the mid-1950s, President Dwight D. Eisenhower, fearing that South Vietnam would choose a Communist form of government, established a military advisory council to create a democratic, U.S.-backed central government. This action prevented South Vietnam from rejoining North Vietnam after years of civil war. North Vietnam had already established Communist ties with the Soviet Union and sought to reunify with the south and establish Communist control of the entire nation.

The United States's first goal was to establish a Vietnamese army to protect the democratic government. U.S. military officials committed personnel, weapons, and training to this army until it became evident in 1965 that the U.S. military would have to take over the bulk of the fighting in order to achieve a victory over the Communists in the northern part of Vietnam.

In 1965 the first protest activities in the United States against the war took place. The university system became the mouthpiece of this movement. Both professors and students conducted teach-ins, which were seminars designed to teach interested protesters about the actions of the U.S. military in Vietnam. Protesters quickly organized marches and mass demonstrations. By 1967 male activists were burning their draft cards in protest against forced service in a war that they did not support. Many fled to Canada, which offered political asylum to Americans wishing to avoid the draft. Although most of the protests were peaceful, in the late sixties, some student demonstrators fought with both police and National Guard units in the streets and sometimes on college campuses over their right to protest the war. On May 4, 1970, National Guard troops fired on Vietnam War protesters at Kent State University, killing four.

In 1971 Congress enacted changes in draft laws that made previously exempt college students, those involved in the full-time pursuit of a bachelor's or postgraduate degree, potential draftees to fight in the war. This move only increased the efforts of protesters searching a quick end to the Vietnam conflict. As Cambridge historian and political scientist D.W. Brogan observed,

> This is the most unpopular war in American history. The belief in victory or even in its morality is ebbing fast; no one believes in victory outside of the Pentagon . . . but it would be uncandid not to note that much of the sudden indignation of the student world [is] due to the sudden decision of the Washington authorities to begin drafting the senior students.[8]

Frustrating the government's attempts to rally support for the war, veterans returning home from Vietnam joined in the antiwar movement in order to prevent others from having to witness the horrors of war in the Vietnamese jungle. By 1970 the Vietnam Veterans Against the War (VVAW) was a vocal unit advocating that the United States withdraw from Vietnam. As veteran John Kerry, who later became a U.S. senator, stated,

> There is nothing in South Vietnam, nothing which could happen that realistically threatens the United States of America. And to attempt to justify the loss of one American life in Vietnam, Cambodia, or Laos by linking such loss to the preservation of freedom, which those misfits supposedly abuse, is to us the height of criminal hypocrisy, and it is that kind of hypocrisy which we feel has torn this country apart.[9]

By 1970 most Americans no longer supported the war. However, the last American soldier would not leave Vietnam until 1975.

THE WOMEN'S LIBERATION MOVEMENT

One of the most significant movements to emerge in the 1960s was the women's liberation movement. The organizers of women's liberation aimed at achieving equality in educational opportunities for women, comparable wages for work, and control over reproductive rights. Before 1960 women did not have much opportunity to take on roles beyond those of housewife or mother. Women who wanted or needed to work but who had not been able to attain higher education had to accept employment in low-wage, low-skilled jobs. Even if a woman had the experience and the education necessary to perform a higher-level job, her compensation for the work was below that of a man with equal education and experience. Women were also not expected to express themselves with the same sexual freedom as men. While it was socially acceptable for a man to have several sex partners, women were still expected to remain sexually pure and were stigmatized if they chose to have sex out of marriage. All of this changed during the sixties.

The introduction of the birth control pill in 1960 contributed greatly to the development of women's liberation. By using the birth control pill, which was claimed to be 99 percent effective in preventing pregnancy, women could now exercise control over their ability to reproduce. Women previously had to worry about the possibility of becoming pregnant, the difficulty of obtaining an illegal abortion, and the social stigma attached to single mothers. This newfound sexual freedom brought by the birth control pill was important to women's liberation because it lowered the rates of unwanted pregnancy and illegal abortions.

Another aspect of the women's liberation movement was the fight for equality in the workplace. In 1964, with the passage of the Title IX provision of the Civil Rights Act outlawing discrimination on the basis of gender, women gained legal grounds to demand wages equal to those earned by men in comparable jobs. This new law created greater opportunities in employment for women in traditionally male-dominated fields such as law, medicine, and business. Although a disparity still existed between the wage-earning potential of women and men, women saw significant increases in wages for jobs requiring similar skills and education. This was an important step in closing the wage disparity gap.

Women in the liberation movement also fought to break free from confining social expectations. In 1963 Betty Friedan published her landmark book *The Feminine Mystique*, which documented the problems women faced in their current societal roles. Her book is often credited with launching the modern feminist movement. According to sixties historian Daniel Horowitz, "*The Feminine Mystique* helped transform the course of America's political and social history."[10] What made Friedan's book popular was its criticism of the dull and narrow life of middle-class suburban housewives and its empowering message that women could change their lives. Friedan addressed the plight of modern women from the initial pages of the book:

> It was a strange stirring, a sense of dissatisfaction, a yearning that women suffered in the middle of the twentieth

century in the United States. Each suburban wife struggled with it alone. As she made the beds, shopped for groceries, matched slipcover material, ate peanut butter sandwiches with her children, chauffeured Cub Scouts and Brownies, lay beside her husband at night—she was afraid to ask even of herself the silent question—Is this all?[11]

Friedan addressed this question as the "problem that has no name" and outlined the common frustrations that many women

Betty Friedan lobbies for equal rights for women. Her landmark book, The Feminine Mystique, *inspired women to break from their traditional roles.*

were feeling about their status as housewives or mothers. By 1966 Friedan had helped to establish the National Organization for Women (NOW), an organization that was essential in pushing forward prochoice legislation on the issue of abortion and educating local communities on issues of reproductive rights.

By 1968 the modern women's movement had separated into two groups: women's liberation and radical feminism. Women's liberation supporters continued to focus on achieving equality with men by removing discriminatory obstacles between men and women. Radical feminists sought to eliminate gender lines completely by attacking the traditional female stereotype that centered on a woman's appearance, sexual appeal, and motherhood. Radical feminism began to develop at the 1968 Miss America Pageant when protesters burned brassieres and carried signs proclaiming that the pageant trapped women in sexual stereotypes. In 1969 the radical feminist group Redstockings was formed in New York City to combat what it viewed as male dominance on all levels of society. Redstockings published *Notes from the Underground*, an influential collection of theoretical papers by emerging feminist scholars. Those articles included Pat Mainardi's *Politics of Housework*, Anne Koedt's *Myth of the Vaginal Orgasm*, and Joreen Freeman's *Bitch Manifesto*, all of which have become standard feminist theoretical documents in college and university courses. In contrast with radical feminism, women's liberation supporters focused on achieving social equality with men, but insisted on maintaining what they viewed as femininity. Women's liberation supporters did not want to sacrifice what they felt were essential aspects of being female. They sought to achieve equality only in educational opportunities, wages, and reproductive rights.

Both groups within the women's movement achieved major victories on the issues of reproductive rights by helping to legalize abortion. They organized hundreds of protest activities to pressure the federal government to repeal antiabortion laws. After much controversy, abortion was legally sanctioned by the Supreme Court on January 22, 1973.

THE SIXTIES DRAW TO A CLOSE

As the sixties drew to a close, the student movement and the counterculture revolution became tarnished by violence, disorganization, and disillusionment. Radical groups of activists broke away from the mainstream protest organizations such as SDS. One such group was the Youth International Party (Yippies), cofounded in 1966 by Abbie Hoffman and Jerry Rubin. Their protest activities were characterized as "guerrilla theater," a public protest that relied heavily on absurd spectacles. The Yippies created media frenzies in almost every major city they visited. The most famous example of their activism was their attempt to elect a pig for president, a candidate dubbed Pigasus. Rubin justified this action by stating that "one pig was as good as another, just like any of today's politicians."[12] The formation of the Yippies and similar extremist groups signaled an impending breakdown within the student movement.

A more radical group was the Weathermen. Journalist David Greenburg states that the group took its name from the lyric in Bob Dylan's song "Subterranean Homesick Blues," which reads "You don't need a weatherman to know which way the wind blows."[13] The Weathermen was one of the most extreme groups to splinter from SDS. Its militant tactics included lighting fires, setting off bombs, and terrorizing innocent citizens. One of its most famous incidents involved an explosion in an apartment in Greenwich Village, a section of New York City. The Weathermen had intended to use the bomb against American soldiers at a local military base, but it went off prematurely, killing three of the bombers. In 1971 the group went into hiding in order to avoid criminal prosecution by the federal government, and changed its name to the Weathermen Underground. Members of the group continued to surface occasionally but remained in hiding until 1980. During the early eighties, they began to turn themselves in as they recognized that their actions were examples of terrorism and did little to further the cause of the New Left.

The sixties were an era marked by idealism and volatility. The combination of domestic and global events during this decade encouraged individuals who might have remained silent on less critical issues to become vocal proponents for civil rights, women's rights, and other issues that affected American society. The counterculture and its student activist component were successful in challenging some of the injustices of American society. By speaking out against the discriminatory practices of the South and by working for civil rights for minorities and women, activists created a lasting impact. Taken together, the various groups of the counterculture movement of the 1960s left a permanent mark on American society.

NOTES

1. John F. Kennedy, "Inaugural Address," January 20, 1961.

2. Fred Davis, "Haight-Ashbury's Hippies and the Future of Society," in *Society as It Is*, eds. Glenn Gaviglio and David E. Raye. New York: Macmillan, 1971, p. 157.

3. Davis, "Haight-Ashbury's Hippies," p. 161.

4. Kate Tuttle, "Medgar Evers," *African American Almanac*, 7th ed. Detroit: Gale, 1997.

5. Quoted in Felicia Kessel, "Jackson: Twenty-Five Years Later," *Crisis*, June/July 1988, p. 22.

6. John Winters, "Sit-Ins." www.ibiblio.org/sncc/sitin.html.

7. H. Rap Brown, *Die Nigger, Die!* New York: Dial Press, 1969, p. 99.

8. D.W. Brogan, "The Student Revolt," *Encounter*, vol. 31, no. 1, July 1968, p. 20.

9. John Kerry, "Vietnam Veterans Against the War," from his speech delivered before the U.S. Senate Committee on Foreign Relations, April 22, 1971.

10. Daniel Horowitz, *Betty Friedan and the Making of* The Feminine Mystique: *The American Left, the Cold War, and Modern Feminism.* Amherst: University of Massachusetts Press, 1998, p. 4.

11. Betty Friedan, *The Feminine Mystique.* New York: Norton, 1963, p. 10.

12. Jerry Rubin, "Inside the Great Pigasus Plot," *Ramparts*, vol. 8, no. 6, December 1969, p. 67.

13. David Greenburg, "Remembering the Weathermen Terrorists," *Slate,* June 9, 2003. www.frontpagemag.com.

CHAPTER 1

THE EARLY STAGES OF AN ANTI-CULTURE

AMERICAN
SOCIAL
MOVEMENTS

The Emergence of the New Left

WINI BREINES

The *New Left* was a term coined to describe the participants of the new liberal movements that appeared on college campuses during the early 1960s. In June 1962 founding members of one of the first groups of the New Left, Students for a Democratic Society (SDS), authored a position paper, the Port Huron Statement, that outlined the goals of the New Left and their desire to implement social change beginning at the university level.

The following selection, by Northwestern University sociology professor Wini Breines, outlines the history of the New Left. Breines first examines the early issues that compelled students in the 1960s to become politically active. She describes this process as difficult because this generation of students lacked mentors to lead them into activism. Breines then explores the ways in which the student movement expanded and changed throughout the 1960s. Breines is the author of several books including *The Great Refusal: Community and Organization in the New Left* and *Young, White, and Miserable: Growing Up Female in the Fifties.*

College and university attendance exploded in the postwar period. There were two million college students in 1950, three million in 1960, five million by 1965 (the first baby boomers were college age in 1964), seven million by 1968 and, by 1973, ten million. In 1970, 50 percent of all people in the United States from eighteen to twenty-two years old were attending college, primarily large public universities. Educational democratization was under way, thanks in part, ironically, to the increasingly tight partnership between the federal government

Wini Breines, "The New Left and the Student Movement," *Long Time Gone: Sixties America Then and Now,* edited by Alexander Bloom. New York: Oxford University Press, 2001. Copyright © 2001 by Alexander Bloom. Reproduced by permission of Oxford University Press, Inc.

and the universities. Federal money poured into the universities, much of which was tied to military-sponsored research. For the first time in American history, masses of young people, female and male, lived together away from their families. I was one of them. In the midst of a growing student population, early white student movement activists often do not stand out from the rest of the conservatively dressed and buttoned-down students in campus photographs. The young men had short hair and wore white shirts, dark trousers, and sometimes even ties. Young women wore skirts. As a girl in the 1950s, I remember having to wear white gloves for dress occasions.

THE 1950S MOLD OF SOCIAL BEHAVIOR

The 1950s were a conservative time in America, and campuses reflected it. The policy of *in loco parentis* meant that college administrators were considered parents away from home—and students were treated like children. At coed and women's institutions this translated into keeping close tabs on undergraduate women through curfews, rules, and strict dormitory life. Young women were not permitted in men's dormitory rooms, and men were not permitted in women's rooms; they socialized in dormitory lobbies and lounges. At my university, if you were in the dormitory lounge with a young man, three out of four of your feet had to be on the ground at all times! Students were expelled if they broke social rules devised to contain and control—and protect—them. Once over Thanksgiving vacation, when the dorms were closed and I had nowhere to stay, I "illegally" stayed in my boyfriend's room in an off-campus men's rooming house. We were reported and both almost expelled. Instead, the dean of men—yes, there was a dean for males and one for females—warned my boyfriend that "a stiff prick knows no conscience," and we were both put on probation. Virginity until marriage was expected of young women, and colleges did their best to enforce it. Ironically, although education has been the path to upward mobility, middle-class white girls' means to security was by earning their "MRS. degree"—finding a husband in college, and, implicitly, the institutions facilitated the project.

Campuses in the 1950s were not political places; college administrators discouraged students from exploring serious politics, and most students were apolitical. Administrators and university trustees often had World War II-related experience and federal government connections, and were politically conservative. They were committed to the dominant Cold War perspective that embraced a notion of the world in which the United States represented the best and most democratic society possible and had a moral and political responsibility to expunge communism. The basic premise was that there was little to be concerned about since everything was good in the United States. The country was strong and prosperous. White families were buying consumer goods, moving to the suburbs, and sending their children to college. From this perspective, what would students have to criticize?

ESTABLISHING A NEW LEFT MOVEMENT

It is difficult to believe that out of this comfortable but conformist and apparently innocent world, a New Left and student movement would develop. Most Americans, including many parents, were shocked when it did. In the years before World War II, especially during the Depression, an old Left centered on the American Communist Party had played an important role in American politics, particularly in organizing unions. But by the 1950s, discredited by vituperative anticommunism and its own internal weaknesses, the old Left was virtually powerless. White youth inaugurated a *New* Left to distinguish their ideas from those of the old Left and to pursue fresh critiques of American society. The most dramatic difference between the old and new Lefts lay in the lack of interest that young people had in the Soviet Union, the site of the first communist revolution and society, and in defending international communism. They were also repelled by postwar–Cold War anti-communism, which they considered irrelevant to solving American social and political problems. Without championing the Soviet Union, they criticized the culture, economy, and politics of the United States.

Some early new leftists did come from old Left families—they were raised by parents who had been, or still were, affiliated with or sympathetic to the American communist movement. The children had grown up in an environment critical of capitalism and of class and racial discrimination in the United States and of the federal government's interventionist and undemocratic foreign policy. From the beginning, then, the New Left, which preceded the student movement, included young people from a variety of backgrounds. All were critical of American society, most were anticapitalist, and many eventually defined themselves as socialist. Over time they developed a position that American capitalism, based on private property and profit, was profoundly undemocratic, and they supported a political vision that ensured, as every individual's right, adequate income, housing, education, and medical care. They came together around local magazines and journals, peace and civil rights activity, the defense of the 1959 Cuban socialist revolution and Fidel Castro, and campus-focused political action groups. One of these was at the University of Michigan, at which Students for a Democratic Society (SDS), the most important new Left student organization in the 1960s, was founded. New leftists were passionately engaged in politics and in developing both a strategic and theoretical understanding of capitalism and socialism, of racism and imperialism. Mainstream Americans considered them utopian, communist, socialist, deviant, or unpatriotic and were disturbed to see student rebels who "should" have been grateful and content. Their student activism sharply contrasted with the mainstream university life of the 1950s—football games, fraternity pranks, and panty raids.

A LACK OF GUIDANCE IN THE NEW LEFT

While they had some mentors, the New Left and student movement were very much invented by young people themselves. They had little choice, for there were few elder leftist leaders or organizations to guide them. At first, most knew little about the history of Left and radical opposition in the United States. Scattered in colleges and universities around the country, only a few professors prodded students to question their society. The Columbia University radical sociologist C. Wright Mills inspired many of the founders of SDS. In *The Power Elite* (1956) Mills argued that an interlocking, powerful elite of the government, corporations, and the military made a mockery of the United States as a democracy. His 1960 "Letter to the New Left" encouraged students to become agents of social change. But the early New Left's central inspiration was the civil rights movement. Throughout the 1950s the movement gathered steam in such struggles as the Montgomery bus boycott and the Little Rock school desegregation battle. Black people had moved young whites with their courage, determination, and dignity. The Student Nonviolent Coordinating Committee (SNCC), the most important youthful and radical civil rights organization of the early 1960s, became a model for the New Left. Although there were civil rights initiatives throughout the 1940s and 1950s, and they had important older mentors—especially SNCC executive director Ella Baker, local activists in southern communities, and Martin Luther King, Jr.—it was the young people who pushed in the direction of radical direct action. . . .

CHANGING SOCIETY BY TRANSFORMING VALUES

The values of the civil rights movement—equality, justice, freedom, and community—transformed the way that many young whites saw their country. They were horrified by racial segregation and discrimination and the recognition of the disparity between the articulated values of American political life and the reality. While official rhetoric spoke of democracy, student activists recognized hypocrisy all around them. Most African Americans were not treated equally, had little opportunity to succeed, and did not receive justice. They were excluded from middle-class prosperity and consumerism and the expectation of secure futures. This contradicted the values that young northern whites had been taught. Young student activists were idealistic. They believed in the values the United States was supposed to stand for, and they embraced John F. Kennedy's rhetoric of hope and civic commitment. Their relatively secure lives, the civil rights movement, and the Kennedy presidency contributed to students' deeply internalized hopes and ideals. That idealism fueled the movements. . . .

One aspect of the New Left that distinguished it from the old Left and traditional politics of all kinds was an effort to link political issues with personal life. Activists recognized that private life was deeply influenced by the organization of power, by economics and culture. Problems that were defined as personal often had social explanations. In addition, they believed that how they lived their lives, in the movement and out, had political implications. In SNCC, the nonviolent "beloved community" consisted of a committed and caring group in the midst of political action; it was this community that provided sustenance in the continuing struggle as well as a model for future relationships. Civil rights workers were building a new society at the same time that they fought to change the old. Influenced by their example, the New Left and student movement attempted to create a political movement that embodied democratic values, a prefigurative politics based on participatory democracy, equality, respect, and community. New leftists, then, were engaged in complicated political work: they were attempting to change society, to understand the influence of politics on personal life, and to create new, less hierarchical, relationships. It was not until the women's liberation movement that this project was fully explored.

THE PORT HURON STATEMENT

Many of these ideas were expressed in the 1962 SDS Port Huron Statement, which has been called "one of the most pivotal documents in postwar American history." It is a long manifesto, written at a retreat in Port Huron, Michigan, primarily by SDS leader Tom Hayden, with help from students from the University of Michigan and other midwestern and eastern SDS chapters. Participants wrote and argued and debated continually, feeling the need to understand and analyze, and to develop theories that informed action. More important than its specific proposals, the Port Huron Statement articulated a sensibility and way of considering the world. . . .

STUDENT ACTIVISTS AND FREE SPEECH

The 1964 free speech movement (FSM) at the Berkeley campus of the University of California is the episode that dramatically brought the student movement into American consciousness. Prior to 1964 the movement had been building around the country, primarily at large state universities in the Midwest and West and on private liberal arts campuses on the East Coast. Small, isolated groups had organized to oppose nuclear bomb testing and advocate peace in the world. The aggressive tactics of the House Un-American Activities Committee, a congressional committee committed to exposing and destroying communism in America, galvanized student protest. The anticommunist, liberal National Student Association had also been active throughout the 1950s. Support groups for SNCC and chapters of northern civil rights organizations grew, and white students went South to participate in freedom rides and voter registration drives. SDS chapters spread throughout the country.

In 1964 Berkeley students became involved in an explosive struggle over their right to engage in politics on campus. That fall the university administration ruled that students could not use the campus to advocate for off-campus political causes, nor to publicize, solicit, raise money for or recruit for political organizations. Prohibitions against raising money for SNCC sparked the student response. A number of FSM leaders had been involved in the civil rights movement and linked the two. At a rally during the free speech movement, leader Mario Savio stated, "Last summer I went to Mississippi to join the struggle there for civil rights. This fall I am engaged in another phase of the same struggle, this time in Berkeley. . . . The same rights are at stake in both places—the right to participate as citizens in democratic society and the right to due process of law. . . . It is a struggle against the same enemy." Students argued that it was a question of constitutional free speech, that they should be able to discuss anything on campus, and questioned who was making decisions and for what reasons. Besides the free speech issue, they rebelled against the top-down and bureaucratic decision making of the administrators who controlled their lives.

When the administration decided to arrest a number of students for violating the ban, the campus erupted. Even students who were not involved in politics supported free speech on campus and were shocked at the summary actions of the administration, which eventually suspended eight students. Several well-publicized demonstrations ensued. During one, students surrounded a police car that held an arrested activist and enthusiastically discussed politics, philosophy, and strategy for thirty-two hours. At another, they occupied the main administration building, Sproul Hall, until the police were called to eject them. Almost eight hundred students risked their academic careers by getting arrested. It was the largest mass arrest in California history. Eventually a majority of the Faculty Senate supported the students against the administration. Through committed and persuasive nonviolent action, the students had succeeded. The ban was rescinded by the university regents. Students were permitted to advocate political causes on the Berkeley campus.

ACTIVISM BECOMES A NATIONAL MOVEMENT

What is most significant about FSM is that it riveted and encouraged students around the country and raised critical issues of politics and strategy that preoccupied the student movement for the rest of the decade. I remember the elation I felt when I heard about FSM in the fall of 1964. I was impressed that students were on the move in California, contributing to what seemed to be becoming a national student movement. I was not alone in being moved by their principled activism:

scores of East Coast students streamed into the Bay Area when they learned about Berkeley radical activism. Themes of participatory democracy, opposition to authoritarian and hierarchical organization, student alienation, student identification with the powerless and those deprived of their rights, disapproval of bureaucracy, and the role of the university as an institution of learning removed from corporate and government interests—all these appeared regularly in speeches and writing from this period and struck responsive chords in students on campuses everywhere.

Throughout the months of FSM a pattern emerged that characterized campus demonstrations throughout the country for years after. Radical students would ask for or demand changes or rights that did not appear to be particularly unreasonable. The university administration would overreact, apparently unable to respond in measured terms to what they considered a threat to their authority. This would mobilize greater numbers of students. The scenario would repeat itself. Eventually the authorities would respond in an extreme manner: suspensions, expulsions, stonewalling, police busts. Discontented students who might never have been mobilized were drawn into the movement. Often they were as outraged at the punitive responses of the university leadership as they were motivated by the issues under consideration. Overreaction on the part of the authorities politicized and radicalized young people, who were particularly sensitive to abuses of power.

The university attempted to discourage discontent—saying, in effect, that campus policy was not debatable. When students undertook nonviolent demonstrations, they were often met by police. Protesters' desire for change was transformed into confrontational struggles as those in power turned hostile to the demonstrators' desire for social change or even for negotiation. This dynamic unfolded in the antiwar movement as it had earlier in the civil rights movement. The civil rights movement began with black people peacefully asking for their rights and escalated into a bloody struggle because of resistance and fury on the part of the authorities attempting to maintain the status quo and their own power. In the case of the war, students began by requesting information about the war in Vietnam, questioning American intentions and attempting to speak to those in power; they received no reasonable response. Peace advocates recognized the same dynamic in the U.S. government's prosecution of the war in Vietnam itself; instead of negotiation, more force was applied. The efforts to "speak truth to power" were not successful in the 1960s.

Student Activism's Evolution Beyond Civil Rights

Distinguishing the New Left from the student movement is difficult. One way to view the development is as an expansion from the New Left, those student intellectuals and activists in the late 1950s and early 1960s who self-consciously saw themselves developing a Left critique of American society, to the larger student movement of the late 1960s, which took on a variety of issues. By the mid-'60s, due in large part to its leadership of the movement against the war in Vietnam, the New Left expanded rapidly into a student movement with tens of thousands of adherents. It centered on SDS and other small pacifist and socialist organizations that wanted more than an end to the war in Vietnam or equality for African Americans. New leftists understood the war in Vietnam as American imperialism, part of a pattern of American intervention in the affairs of other, usually Third World, countries. Many became socialists. But most of those who "joined" or identified with the student movement in the second half of the 1960s were not new leftists. They were not generally engaged in thinking about socialism or revolution, community organizing, exposing corporate liberalism, or consciously fighting against capitalist institutions. The newer participants were more likely to be against the war in Vietnam and angry and frustrated with the narrowness of the norms and values of American society. They were antiauthoritarian, suspicious of leaders and experts, and discontented with the roles and rules set out for young people.

Another way of thinking about the distinction is in terms of movement generations. Those who were twenty years old in Ann Arbor in 1961, where SDS was founded, for example, were twenty-nine in 1970, while thousands of young people, a decade or more younger, had become active by the end of the decade. As increasing numbers of lower-middle-class and working-class students identified with the student and antiwar movements and younger people, including high school students, joined, the student movement became more heterogeneous. The younger activists were usually galvanized by Vietnam, the Black Power movement, the counterculture, repressive high school or campus regulations, or an interest in drugs, sex, and rock 'n' roll. Unlike older new leftists, they were even less interested in and more suspicious of organized and institutionalized politics because they had come of age as the government was being discredited by its brutal policies at home and in Vietnam and by the social movements against it.

Another point is worth making. While confrontations at Berkeley in 1964, Columbia University in 1968, San Francisco State in 1969, and Kent State in 1970 were among the most significant student movement events of the 1960s, students throughout the country grew increasingly active, on campuses small and large, rural and urban, at community colleges and religious institutions, both private and public. They often did not receive the media attention beamed at the large major public universities and elite colleges, but upheaval was everywhere. It was a social movement precisely because so many students were in motion.

CONNECTING THE NEW LEFT TO THE COUNTERCULTURE

Finally, the relationship between the student movement and counterculture can not be ignored. The American youth movement was accompanied and constituted by political popular music. Folk music, rhythm and blues, soul, Motown, and rock drew in young people and contributed to their sense of separateness from mainstream America and the adult world.

The generational rupture is suggested by Bob Dylan's lyric from the "Ballad of a Thin Man": "Something is happening, and you don't know what it is, do you, Mr. Jones?" Dylan and Joan Baez, to mention only the most famous young folk musicians, sang songs of social significance, some of which, like "Blowin' in the Wind," became radical anthems. Rock 'n' roll lyrics were increasingly political, articulating antiwar and racial themes, and confrontational in their endorsement of youth culture, particularly drugs. From folk music and blues in the late 1950s and early 1960s to the Beatles, Janis Joplin, Marvin Gaye, the Doors, the Grateful Dead, Sly and the Family Stone, James Brown and numerous others, music spoke to and for dissident young people.

It is inaccurate if not impossible to separate interwoven strands of rebellion and opposition. In the midst of growing concerns about Vietnam, the "summer of love" unfolded in 1967. Young people flocked to the Haight Ashbury section of San Francisco and other counterculture enclaves in college towns across America. Accompanied by the new rock music, they experimented with sex and drugs. They created and identified with a youth culture that rejected conformity, materialism, war, delayed gratification, and destruction of the earth. Concerned with more than traditional party politics, young people questioned social roles of all sorts. Asking who they were and who they wanted to be, they embarked on a journey of deprogramming themselves from mainstream norms. A youth revolt of vast proportions was under way. Political movements of the late 1960s were infused with lifestyle explorations, and although there were clear demarcations between hippies and political activists, elements of each were adopted by the other. The separation between the political movements and the counterculture was never neat. Student activists often identified with both political and cultural rebellion. SDSers and new leftists kept their focus on politics, particularly the war, but many were engaged in cultural revolution too. They changed their style of dress, grew their hair long, smoked marijuana, experimented with LSD, and explored sexual relationships. The well-groomed young radicals of the early 1960s were nowhere to be seen by 1967. Photographs from the time show my New Left husband, a graduate student who had pledged a fraternity in his freshman year, with long hair and bell bottoms. The New Left became the student movement and the student movement became the antiwar movement—and the counterculture affected nearly everyone involved.

Introduction to the Port Huron Statement

STUDENTS FOR A DEMOCRATIC SOCIETY

Beginning in 1960, an increasing number of white student activists became organizers in Mississippi and Alabama, working to remove civil rights barriers against blacks. Future student activist leaders such as Tom Hayden and Staughton Lynd worked alongside southern blacks to integrate lunch counters, restrooms, and public transportation in the segregated South. Black and white activists also worked together to remove legal barriers that prevented blacks from exercising their constitutional right to vote.

In June 1962, after several months of meetings and preparations, Hayden and several other student activists organized a national convention for the formation of a new political group to be called Students for a Democratic Society (SDS). Their goal was to motivate young people to political activism. Their training ground was to be the nation's university system, in which young people would learn to challenge antidemocratic social and political policies. In this introduction to the Port Huron Statement, issued on June 15 at the SDS National Convention in Port Huron, Michigan, the student leaders outline the country's major social problems and the philosophical reasons for confronting these issues.

We are people of this generation, bred in at least modest comfort, housed now in universities, looking uncomfortably to the world we inherit.

When we were kids the United States was the wealthiest and strongest country in the world: the only one with the atom

Students for a Democratic Society, "Introduction: Agenda for a Generation," *The Port Huron Statement*, http://lists.village.virginia.edu/sixties, 1999. Copyright © 1962 by Tom Hayden. Reproduced by permission.

bomb, the least scarred by modern war, an initiator of the United Nations that we thought would distribute Western influence throughout the world. Freedom and equality for each individual, government of, by, and for the people—these American values we found [good], principles by which we could live as men. Many of us began maturing in complacency.

As we grew, however, our comfort was penetrated by events too troubling to dismiss. First, the permeating and victimizing fact of human degradation, symbolized by the Southern struggle against racial bigotry, compelled most of us from silence to activism. Second, the enclosing fact of the Cold War, symbolized by the presence of the Bomb, brought awareness that we ourselves, and our friends, and millions of abstract "others" we knew more directly because of our common peril, might die at any time. We might deliberately ignore, or avoid, or fail to feel all other human problems, but not these two, for these were too immediate and crushing in their impact, too challenging in the demand that we as individuals take the responsibility for encounter and resolution.

THE EQUALITY PARADOX

While these and other problems either directly oppressed us or rankled our consciences and became our own subjective concerns, we began to see complicated and disturbing paradoxes in our surrounding America. The declaration "all men are created equal . . ." rang hollow before the facts of Negro life in the South and the big cities of the North. The proclaimed peaceful intentions of the United States contradicted its economic and military investments in the Cold War status quo.

We witnessed, and continue to witness, other paradoxes. With nuclear energy whole cities can easily be powered, yet the dominant nation-states seem more likely to unleash destruction greater than that incurred in all wars of human history. Although our own technology is destroying old and creating new forms of social organization, men still tolerate meaningless work and idleness. While two-thirds of mankind suffers undernourishment, our own upper classes revel amidst superfluous abundance. Although world population is expected to double in forty years, the nations still tolerate anarchy as a major principle of international conduct and uncontrolled exploitation governs the sapping of the earth's physical resources. Although mankind desperately needs revolutionary leadership, America rests in national stalemate, its goals ambiguous and tradition-bound instead of informed and clear, its democratic system apathetic and manipulated rather than "of, by, and for the people. . . ."

A NEED FOR REFORM ALTERNATIVES

Our work is guided by the sense that we may be the last generation in the experiment with living. But we are a minority—the vast majority of our people regard the temporary equilibriums of our society and world as eternally functional parts. In this is perhaps the outstanding paradox; we ourselves are imbued with urgency, yet the message of our society is that there is no viable alternative to the present. Beneath the reassuring tones of the politicians, beneath the common opinion that America will "muddle through," beneath the stagnation of those who have closed their minds to the future, is the pervading feeling that there simply are no alternatives, that our times have witnessed the exhaustion not only of Utopias, but of any new departures as well. Feeling the press of complexity upon the emptiness of life, people are fearful of the thought that at any moment things might be thrust out of control. They fear change itself, since change might smash whatever invisible framework seems to hold back chaos for them now. For most Americans, all crusades are suspect, threatening. The fact that each individual sees apathy in his fellows perpetuates the common reluctance to organize for change. The dominant institutions are complex enough to blunt the minds of their potential critics, and entrenched enough to swiftly dissipate or entirely repel the energies of protest and reform, thus limiting human expectancies. Then, too, we are a materially improved society, and by our own improvements we seem to have weakened the case for further change.

Some would have us believe that Americans feel contentment amidst prosperity—but might it not better be called a glaze above deeply felt anxieties about their role in the new world? And if these anxieties produce a developed indifference to human affairs, do they not as well produce a yearning to believe that there *is* an alternative to the present, that something *can* be done to change circumstances in the school, the workplaces, the bureaucracies, the government? It is to this latter yearning, at once the spark and engine of change, that we direct our present appeal. The search for truly democratic alternatives to the present, and a commitment to social experimentation with them, is a worthy and fulfilling human enterprise, one which moves us and, we hope, others today. On such a basis do we offer this document of our convictions and analysis: as an effort in understanding and changing the conditions of humanity in the late twentieth century, an effort rooted in the ancient, still unfulfilled conception of man attaining determining influence over his circumstances of life.

CORRUPTION IN THE CURRENT VALUE SYSTEM

Making values explicit—an initial task in establishing alternatives—is an activity that has been devalued and corrupted. The conventional moral terms of the age, the politician moralities—"free world," "people's democracies"—reflect realities poorly, if at all, and seem to function more as ruling myths than as descriptive principles. But neither has our experience in the universities brought us moral enlightenment. Our professors and administrators sacrifice controversy to public relations; their curriculums change more slowly than the living events of the world; their skills and silence are purchased by investors in the arms race; passion is called unscholastic. The questions we might want raised—what is really important? can we live in a different and better way? if we wanted to change society, how would we do it?—are not thought to be questions of a "fruitful, empirical nature," and thus are brushed aside.

Unlike youth in other countries we are used to moral leadership being exercised and moral dimensions being clarified by our elders. But today, for us, not even the liberal and socialist preachments of the past seem adequate to the forms of the present. . . .

In suggesting social goals and values, therefore, we are aware of entering a sphere of some disrepute. Perhaps matured by the past, we have no formulas, no closed theories—but that does not mean values are beyond discussion and tentative determination. A first task of any social movement is to convince people that the search for orienting theories and the creation of human values is complex but worthwhile. We are aware that to avoid platitudes we must analyze the concrete conditions of social order. But to direct such an analysis we must use the guideposts of basic principles. Our own social values involve conceptions of human beings, human relationships, and social systems.

REAFFIRMING HUMANITY'S POTENTIAL

We regard *men* as infinitely precious and possessed of unfulfilled capacities for reason, freedom, and love. In affirming these principles we are aware of countering perhaps the dominant conceptions of man in the twentieth century: that he is a thing to be manipulated, and that he is inherently incapable of directing his own affairs. We oppose the depersonalization that reduces human being to the status of things—if anything, the brutalities of the twentieth century teach that means and ends are intimately related, that vague appeals to "posterity" cannot justify the mutilations of the present. We oppose, too, the doctrine of human incompetence because it rests essentially on the modern fact that men have been "competently" manipulated into incompetence—we see little reason why men cannot meet with increasing skill the complexities and responsibilities of their situation, if society is organized not for minority, but for majority, participation in decision-making.

Men have unrealized potential for self-cultivation, self-direction, self-understanding, and creativity. It is this potential that we regard as crucial and to which we appeal, not to the human potentiality for violence, unreason, and submission to authority. The goal of man and society should be human independence: a concern not with image of popularity but with finding a meaning in life that is personally authentic; a quality of mind not compulsively driven by a sense of powerlessness, nor one which unthinkingly adopts status values, nor one which represses all threats to its habits, but one which has full, spontaneous access to present and past experiences, one which easily unites the fragmented parts of personal history, one which openly faces problems which are troubling and unresolved; one with an intuitive awareness of possibilities, an active sense of curiosity, an ability and willingness to learn. . . .

ENCOURAGING NEW PRINCIPLES OF PARTICIPATORY DEMOCRACY

We would replace power rooted in possession, privilege, or circumstance by power and uniqueness rooted in love, reflectiveness, reason, and creativity. As a social system we seek the establishment of a democracy of individual participation, governed by two central aims: that the individual share in those social decisions determining the quality and direction of his life; that society be organized to encourage independence in men and provide the media for their common participation.

> In a participatory democracy, the political life would be based in several root principles: that decision-making of basic social consequence be carried on by public groupings;
>
> that politics be seen positively, as the art of collectively creating an acceptable pattern of social relations;
>
> that politics has the function of bringing people out of isolation and into community, thus being a necessary, though not sufficient, means of finding meaning in personal life;
>
> that the political order should serve to clarify problems in a way instrumental to their solution; it should provide outlets for the expression of personal grievance and aspiration; opposing views should be organized so as to illuminate choices

and facilitate the attainment of goals; channels should be commonly available to relate men to knowledge and to power so that private problems—from bad recreation facilities to personal alienation—are formulated as general issues.

The economic sphere would have as its basis the principles:

that work should involve incentives worthier than money or survival. It should be educative, not stultifying; creative, not mechanical; self-directed, not manipulated, encouraging independence, a respect for others, a sense of dignity, and a willingness to accept social responsibility, since it is this experience that has crucial influence on habits, perceptions and individual ethics;

that the economic experience is so personally decisive that the individual must share in its full determination;

that the economy itself is of such social importance that its major resources and means of production should be open to democratic participation and subject to democratic social regulation. . . .

These are our central values, in skeletal form. It remains vital to understand their denial or attainment in the context of the modern world.

Participatory Democracy and the Concept of Community

STAUGHTON LYND

Staughton Lynd earned a Ph.D. in history from Columbia University and spent much of the early 1960s teaching in black universities. By 1963 he was actively involved in the freedom schools of Atlanta, all-black schools run by student activists who aimed to provide blacks with an education equal to that offered to white students. Lynd also spent much of his time organizing civil rights protests. By 1965 he was teaching history at Yale University and working to establish an antiwar movement there. In this selection, Lynd examines the principles of participatory democracy outlined by the Port Huron Statement of the SDS. He explains that ideally people in a participatory democracy can develop a parallel system of social programs that can effectively compete with existing social programs put in place by the dominant system of government. He states that this is not economically possible, however, as grassroots movements do not have the financial resources to compete with the federal government. Thus, he argues, grassroots organizations should work with the government to help the poor in the community and to make sure that benefits are distributed fairly. In practice, as the 1960s counterculture developed, activists within the movement often clashed with the system they were working within, making it difficult to address the needs of the community.

Staughton Lynd, "The New Radicals and Participatory Democracy," *Dissent,* vol. 12, Summer 1965, pp. 324–33. Copyright © 1965 by Dissent Publishing Corporation. Reproduced by permission.

W hat is the strategy of social change implicit in the concept of participatory democracy? What is its relation
to older philosophies of the Left: socialism, nonviolence, an-
archism? As one distant from the scene I offer the following
observations diffidently, in the hope that they will comment
from "participatory democrats," North and South.

One aspect of participatory democracy is the idea of parallel structures. The FDP [Freedom Democratic Party] is a parallel political party, prompted by the conclusion that registration of Negroes in the regular Democratic party of Mississippi
is presently impossible. Freedom Schools[1] were parallel schools,
although delegates to the Freedom School Convention decided they would return to the public schools and seek to
transform them rather than continue into the winter a parallel school system. In the North, neighborhood unions organized by SDS [Students for a Democratic Society] represent
parallel antipoverty agencies, challenging the legitimacy of the
top-down middle-class "community organizations" sponsored
by urban renewal and antipoverty administrators.

COEXISTENCE VS. REPLACEMENT OF SOCIAL SYSTEMS

The intent of these structures is still unclear, even to those involved in organizing them. There is a spectrum of possibilities. At one end of the spectrum is the concept of using parallel institutions to transform their Establishment counterparts.
Thus it would follow that when Mississippi Negroes *can* register and vote, the FDP would wither away. At the spectrum's
other end is the conviction that in an America whose Establishment is inherently and inevitably hostile, existing institutions cannot be transformed, participation will always mean
cooptation and merely token successes, hence parallel institutions must survive and grow into an anti-Establishment network, a new society.

For the moment participatory democracy cherishes the

1. all-black schools set up in southern states by activist organizations in order to provide
an equal education to white schools

practice of parallelism as a way of saying No to organized America, and of initiating the unorganized into the experience of self-government. The SNCC [Student Nonviolent Coordinating Committee] or SDS worker does not build a parallel institution to impose an ideology on it. He views himself as a catalyst, helping to create an environment which will help the local people to decide what they want. Recognizing himself as a part of the society's sickness, the organizer inclines to regard the unorganized poor as purer than himself. There is an unstated assumption that the poor, when they find voice, will produce a truer, sounder radicalism than any which alienated intellectuals might prescribe. In the meantime the very existence of the parallel institution is felt to be a healthier and more genuine experience than any available alternative. It seems better to sit in the back of the room in silent protest against the bureaucrats up front than to seek to elect a man to join the executive committee. . . .

I for one believe that participatory democracy, even thus vaguely conceived, offers a growing point far more alive than conventional coalition politics. At the same time, it is incumbent upon new radicals to explain how they propose to answer the problems which conventional politics purports to solve. How will participatory democracy feed and clothe the poor, as well as stimulate and involve them? If voting is a snare and a delusion, what is not? Unless in time these questions can be answered participatory democracy could become a subtle, even if heroic, form of self-indulgence.

THE ECONOMIC LIMITATIONS OF PARTICIPATORY DEMOCRACY

Employment appears to be the Achilles heel of parallelism. From time to time SNCC workers have sought to organize producers and consumers cooperatives, and the leather-working business in Haywood and Fayette counties, Tennessee, has had considerable success. The thriving toy business of the Society of Brothers (Bruderhof) proves that even in the age of monopoly a small cooperative enterprise can survive. But one cannot imagine such economic beginnings becoming, like the free cities of the Middle Ages, the "germ of a new society within the womb of the old." In Mississippi the movement has hardly been able to provide for Negroes fired as a result of civil rights activity, let alone address itself to the larger problem of cotton-picking machinery and the displacement of farm labor; and what provision there has been has come, not through the creation of a new economic base, but from charity.

It would seem, therefore, that in the area of economics participatory democracy cannot provide a full alternative to established institutions except by capturing and transforming them. By pressure it can democratize the distribution of income, as SDS does in boring-from-below against antipoverty programs, as SNCC does in demanding the participation of Negroes in local committees sponsored by the Department of Agriculture. . . . But can we not agree that participatory democracy, understood as a movement building new institutions side-by-side with the old, cannot provide bread and land? Failure to face this problem realistically will result in the poor turning for help to those who can provide it at least in part, and the cooptation of protest movements by the Establishment. . . .

CREATING MORE THAN A TEMPORARY SOLUTION

Some common ground, some underlying vision needs to be articulated which genuinely unites socialism and "participatory democracy," which challenges each to transcend itself. Here one strikes out into unexplored territory which can only be adequately clarified by experience. A helpful starting point may be the concept of "community." "Politics," affirms the Port Huron Statement, "has the function of bringing people out of isolation and into community." And [writer and historian] A.J. Muste writes, correctly I think, of the civil rights movement:

> No one can have a fairly close contact with the civil rights movement and the people in it, including the young people, without feeling that in spite of all contrary appearances and

even realities in the movement, deep near its center is this aspiration for a blessed community and the faith that this is what they are working for and already in a sense realizing now.

Community was what one Freedom School teacher meant who wrote to me: "The summer project presented itself to us as a potentially life-endangering situation, and so we all worked our fears out together, which gave coherence to our group. We had temporarily put aside our human fears and were accepting a responsibility which was ours and we were doing it together."

THE POLITICAL MEANING OF COMMUNITY

Lest this seem maudlin utopianism, let us begin with the most hard-headed meaning of community to a new radical movement: the political. How can one build a political campaign, or a political party, without sacrificing the shared intimacy experienced in a direct action "project"? If it be true that both peace and civil rights activists must turn toward politics to cope with the economic problems which confront their movements, can it be done without losing the spiritual exaltation of the direct action years?

I think a clue here is to begin to think of politics as administration. Political representation was devised as a mechanism to obtain consent for taxation. It is an institutional process peculiarly appropriate to an economy in which production is in private hands, and the state takes money from the citizen to spend it on a separate category of public activities. In a communal economy—by which I simply mean an economy wherein men share the fruits of their labor in the spirit of a family—many functions, now centralized in private hands, would be centralized in the hands of the government; but also, many functions now locally privatized would at once become neighborly responsibilities. Consider urban renewal. If land were publicly owned and building a public function, slum clearance could really become a process in which the people of a site participated at each stage. Nation- and city-wide considerations would enter in, of course: but much that now happens in public and private offices on upper floors could then be left to the collective discretion of neighborhood meetings.

THE IMPORTANCE OF COMMUNITY OPPORTUNITIES

In centering its attention on grass roots participation in urban renewal and antipoverty programs, rather than on running candidates, SDS appears instinctively to recognize the communal opportunities of public economic administration. As more and more candidates begin to run for public office on a movement platform, so also new forms of direct action will be improvised to democratize administration; and as regional and national coordination takes form in the one area, so will it in the other, too. Thus entrance into politics need *not* mean an abandonment of direct action demonstration, nor of its spirit. . . .

The local project can grow from protest into administration; if necessary it could also be the building block for resistance to more extreme forms of repression, for protest against Fascism. Like a biological cell it can take many forms, responding in a variety of appropriate ways to alternate stimuli from the environment.

But for this to be so it becomes necessary to think of a project from the beginning, not merely as a tool for social change, but as a community. The community is made up both of people from the neighborhood and of staff persons who, on a long-term basis, so far as they can become part of the neighborhood. The spirit of a community, as opposed to an organization, is not, We are together to accomplish this or that end, but, We are together to face together whatever life brings.

TWO RULES FOR BUILDING COMMUNITY

The experience of Utopian or "intentional" communities suggests certain ground rules which all groups seeking to live as brothers should consider. One is: It is important to be honest with each other, to carry grievances directly to those concerned rather than to third parties. Another is: The spiritual unity of the group is more important than any external accomplishment, and time must be taken to discover and restore that unity even at the cost of short-run tangible failures.

If indeed, as Marxism affirms, mankind will one day enter a realm of freedom that will permit men to guide their behavior by more humane and immediate criteria than the minimum and maximum demands of political programs, the work of transition can begin now. The need for structural change (socialism) should neither be ignored nor overemphasized. Provided we do not deceive ourselves as to the bleakness of our society's prospects for hopeful change or the catastrophic dangers of nuclear war and domestic totalitarianism, perhaps it is not unreasonable to look for a more firm and definite strategy to develop as the collective experience of the movement unfolds.

In sum, then, participatory democracy seems to be driving toward the "live-in," the building of a brotherly way of life even in the jaws of Leviathan. It is conscientious objection [opposition from a philosophical standpoint] not just to war, but to the whole fabric of a dehumanized society. It is civil disobedience not just by individuals, but, hopefully, by broad masses of alienated Americans. Like the conscientious objector, however, the participatory democrat has unfinished business with the question: Is what's intended a moral gesture only, or a determined attempt to transform the American power structure?

A Free Speech Challenge

Mario Savio

By 1964 student activist groups were establishing chapters on college campuses throughout the nation. At the University of California, Berkeley, student activist groups such as the Student Nonviolent Coordinating Committee (SNCC) and Students for a Democratic Society (SDS) were told by the university administration that they could no longer stage political rallies or demonstrations on university property. Berkeley students challenged the right of the university to control political demonstrations, and precedent-setting clashes followed.

Mario Savio, a philosophy student at Berkeley, helped to organize the Free Speech Movement (FSM). Using techniques he had learned during voter registration drives in Mississippi and Alabama, Savio organized several sit-ins and other acts of nonviolent protest to challenge university officials. These nonviolent protests typified the political activism of the counterculture. This selection is from a speech Savio delivered at a sit-in at Berkeley's Sproul Hall in 1964. Savio states that students have a responsibility to defy accepted laws and procedures if those laws act as an obstacle to equality.

L ast summer I went to Mississippi to join the struggle there for civil rights. This fall I am engaged in another phase of the same struggle, this time in Berkeley. The two battlefields may seem quite different to some observers, but this is not the case. The same rights are at stake in both places—the right to participate as citizens in democratic society and the right to due process of law. Further, it is a struggle against the same enemy. In Mississippi an autocratic and powerful minority rules, through organized violence, to suppress the vast, virtually pow-

Mario Savio, "The End of History," *Humanity*, December 1964. Copyright © 1964 by *Humanity*. Reproduced by permission.

erless majority. In California, the privileged minority manipulates the university bureaucracy to suppress the students' political expression. That "respectable" bureaucracy masks the financial plutocrats; that impersonal bureaucracy is the efficient enemy in a "Brave New World."

STANDING AGAINST THE STATUS QUO

In our free-speech fight at the University of California, we have come up against what may emerge as the greatest problem of our nation—depersonalized, unresponsive bureaucracy. We have encountered the organized status quo in Mississippi, but it is the same in Berkeley. Here we find it impossible usually to meet with anyone but secretaries. Beyond that, we find functionaries who cannot make policy but can only hide behind the rules. We have discovered total lack of response on the part of the policy makers. To grasp a situation which is truly Kafkaesque [a reference to author Franz Kafka], it is necessary to understand the bureaucratic mentality. And we have learned quite a bit about it this fall, more outside the classroom than in.

As bureaucrat, an administrator believes that nothing new happens. He occupies an a-historical point of view. In September [1964], to get the attention of this bureaucracy which had issued arbitrary edicts suppressing student political expression and refused to discuss its action, we held a sit-in on the campus. We sat around a police car and kept it immobilized for over thirty-two hours. At last, the administrative bureaucracy agreed to negotiate. But instead, on the following Monday, we discovered that a committee had been appointed, in accordance with usual regulations, to resolve the dispute. Our attempt to convince any of the administrators that an event had occurred, that something new had happened, failed. They saw this simply as something to be handled by normal university procedures.

The same is true of all bureaucracies. They begin as tools, means to certain legitimate goals, and they end up feeding their own existence. The conception that bureaucrats have is that history has in fact come to an end. No events can occur now that the Second World War is over which can change American society substantially. We proceed by standard procedures as we are.

Rejecting Historical Judgments About the Dispossessed

The most crucial problems facing the United States today are the problem of automation and the problem of racial injustice. Most people who will be put out of jobs by machines will not accept an end to events, this historical plateau, as the point beyond which no change occurs. Negroes will not accept an end to history here. All of us must refuse to accept history's final judgment that in America there is no place in society for people whose skins are dark. On campus students are not about to accept it as fact that the university has ceased evolving and is in its final state of perfection, that students and faculty are respectively raw material and employees, or that the university is to be autocratically run by unresponsive bureaucrats.

Here is the real contradiction: the bureaucrats hold history as ended. As a result significant parts of the population both on campus and off are dispossessed and these dispossessed are not about to accept this a-historical point of view. It is out of this that the conflict has occurred with the university bureaucracy and will continue to occur until that bureaucracy becomes responsive or until it is clear the university cannot function.

Asking for Basic Rights

The things we are asking for in our civil-rights protests have a deceptively quaint ring. We are asking for the due process of law. We are asking for our actions to be judged by committees of our peers. We are asking that regulations ought to be considered as arrived at legitimately only from the consensus of the governed. These phrases are all pretty old, but they are not being taken seriously in America today, nor are they being taken seriously on the Berkeley campus.

I have just come from a meeting with the Dean of Students. She notified us that she was aware of certain violations of university regulations by certain organizations. University Friends of Student Non-violent Coordinating Committee, which I represent, was one of these. We tried to draw from her some statement on these great principles, consent of the governed, jury of one's peers, due process. The best she could do was to evade or to present the administration party line. It is very hard to make any contact with the human being who is behind these organizations.

The university is the place where people begin seriously to question the conditions of their existence and raise the issue of whether they can be committed to the society they have been born into. After a long period of apathy during the fifties, students have begun not only to question but, having arrived at answers, to act on those answers. This is part of a growing understanding among many people in America that history has not ended, that a better society is possible, and that it is worth dying for.

This free-speech fight points up a fascinating aspect of contemporary campus life. Students are permitted to talk all they want so long as their speech has no consequences.

Contrasting Views of the University

One conception of the university, suggested by a classical Christian formulation, is that it be in the world but not of the world. The conception of [Berkeley chancellor] Clark Kerr by contrast is that the university is part and parcel of this particular stage in the history of American society; it stands to serve the need of American industry; it is a factory that turns out a certain product needed by industry or government. Because speech does often have consequences which might alter this perversion of higher education, the university must put itself in a position of censorship. It can permit two kinds of speech, speech which encourages continuation of the status quo, and speech which advocates changes in it so radical as to be irrelevant in the foreseeable future. Someone may advocate radical change in all aspects of American society, and this I am sure he can do with impunity. But if someone advocates sit-ins to bring about changes in discriminatory hiring practices, this cannot be permitted because it goes against the status quo of which the university is a part. And that is how the fight began here.

The administration of the Berkeley campus has admitted that external, extra-legal groups have pressured the university not to permit students on campus to organize picket lines, not to permit on campus any speech with consequences. And the bureaucracy went along. Speech with consequences, speech in the area of civil rights, speech which some might regard as illegal, must stop.

THE BLEAK FUTURE OF THE CURRENT STUDENT

Many students here at the university, many people in society, are wandering aimlessly about. Strangers in their own lives, there is no place for them. They are people who have not learned to compromise, who for example have come to the university to learn to question, to grow, to learn—all the standard things that sound like cliches because no one takes them seriously. And they find at one point or other that for them to become part of society, to become lawyers, ministers, businessmen, people in government, that very often they must compromise those principles which were most dear to them. They must suppress the most creative impulses that they have; this is a prior condition for being part of the system. The university is well structured, well tooled, to turn out people with all the sharp edges worn off, the well-rounded person. The university is well equipped to produce that sort of person, and this means that the best among the people who enter must for four years wander aimlessly much of the time questioning why they are on campus at all, doubting whether there is any point in what they are doing, and looking toward a very bleak existence afterward in a game in which all of the rules have been made up, which one cannot really amend.

It is a bleak scene, but it is all a lot of us have to look forward to. Society provides no challenge. American society in the standard conception it has of itself is simply no longer exciting.

The most exciting things going on in America today are movements to change America. America is becoming ever more the utopia of sterilized, automated contentment. The "futures" and "careers" for which American students now prepare are for the most part intellectual and moral wastelands. This chrome-plated consumers' paradise would have us grow up to be well-behaved children. But an important minority of men and women coming to the front today have shown that they will die rather than be standardized, replaceable and irrelevant.

CHAPTER 2

IDENTITY, MUSIC, AND DRUGS IN MID-1960s HIPPIE CULTURE

AMERICAN
SOCIAL
MOVEMENTS

The Anti-Achiever

JESSE R. PITTS

During the 1960s the hippie culture developed out of the burgeoning protest movements against conservative political ideologies and social mores. Led by student activists, a subculture emerged that opposed the mainstream measures of success established by their parents in the 1950s. Most hippies embraced long hair, casual drug use, psychedelic music and fashion, and pacifism. Most rejected traditional means of gainful employment. Many hippies moved into communes, private communities based on utopian or antimaterialist ideals. Many hippies also flocked to large cities where protest demonstrations were centered. In this essay, author Jesse R. Pitts, an active member of Students for a Democratic Society, argues that the hippie lifestyle fundamentally reinforces American idealism. Pitts contends that the hippie belief in independence, self-determination, and love is an extension of the values set forth by America's Puritan heritage. Thus, in Pitts's view, the hippie represents America's most basic values and challenges a morally corrupt system of government, much like the American forefathers did during America's birth as a nation.

Hippies seem to fascinate the mass media somewhat less than they did a year or two ago. But they have not disappeared. Older Hippies, who refused to reconvert to straight society, have moved from [San Francisco's] Haight Ashbury to Big Sur [California] or other places more removed from the tourist trade. "Communes" [communities founded on Socialist principles] have sprung up in rural or urban settings, and Hippies are less noticeable now that some of their fashions have become part of youth culture. Some say that Hippies have become Yippies: they have renounced nonviolence and

Jesse R. Pitts, "The Hippies as Contrameritocracy," *Dissent*, vol. 14, July/August 1969, pp. 326–37. Copyright © 1969 by Dissent Publishing Corporation. Reproduced by permission.

66 • THE COUNTERCULTURE MOVEMENT OF THE 1960s

political indifference in favor of active provocation and resistance. Others say the Yippies are an invention of the mass media. The "mother-fucker" wing of SDS [Students for a Democratic Society] seems to consist of "Hipster"-type Hippies attracted by the pornography of violence.

But regardless of the vagaries of fashion that permit successive cohorts of youth to differentiate themselves from one another, the Hippie phenomenon seems here to stay, not merely as a variety of the perennial bohemian fringe well described some years ago by [writer] Ned Polsky in this magazine [*Dissent*], but as a social movement of some significance.

A NEW CLASS OF ANTIACHIEVERS

It is likely that Hippies, ostentatiously doing their thing even in Traverse City, Michigan, are an intrinsic part of the post-industrial world. My hypothesis is that there is developing in the United States (and probably in other industrialized countries of the West) a *contrameritocracy* which offers the failures or dropouts of the achievement society a haven that neutralizes the pains of failure. Until now this antiachievement society was located either at the very top or bottom. At the upper-class level we had "café society," at the bottom disorganized working-class elements and hoboes. (The underworld, by contrast, has an achievement orientation.) By its nature, the upper class cannot endorse the achievement criteria of the middle class. It must shift the grounds of status from occupational achievement to family-rooted superiorities: ancientness of dynasty, graceful living, and a commitment to *noblesse oblige.* Style is more important than the consequences of action. The upper class also supports the more high-brow forms of art; for this appreciation seems to require special gifts not available to conventional middle-class patrons. In its struggle against the middle class it is often led to disparage the values of hard work, thrift, and personal restraint in favor of an ethic of prowess flowing from inherent traits of personality ("breeding"). The "Jet Set" is the militant expression of the antiachievement aspect of the upper-class ethos.

In the past few years, however, the Jet Set has become more and more a transmission belt into some sections of the middle class for fashions, mannerisms, and ideology originating mainly in the Hippie movement. This is because the Hippie movement has become the effective center of the contrameritocracy in the United States and probably also in England, though in Japan, Germany, Italy, and France, New Left patterns have been more important. The New Left copes with the threat of failure by asserting that opportunity for achievement does not really exist, since it is monopolized by a nation's power elite. The Hippie movement claims that the opportunities offered by the meritocracy must not be pursued if man is to save his soul. It has become the effective center of the contrameritocracy, because its values and behavior patterns permit a thorough and enthusiastic alienation, and because its critique, whatever its "scientific" value, offers a disturbing challenge to society.

It is my contention that the Hippie movement is made up of youths who are overcommitted to the basic middle-class values but are unwilling to realize those values in the occupational world. Since their attachment to middle-class values makes them unwilling to enter the world of juvenile delinquency, there remain for them the patterns of heroic value commitment and expressive behavior, through which they align their stand with that of the upper class—but without the latter's devotion to graceful living and essential conservatism. The Hippie movement is a religious sect through which the members reach what they feel to be the highest levels of value achievement, and thus they attempt to bring salvation to the corrupt society that rejects them. The use of the adjective "religious" is justified by the constant reference in the Hippie movement to nonrational, nonempirical forces, its concern with the ultimate ends and meanings of life, and its relative immunity to organizational failure. To describe the Hippie movement as "religious" is also warranted by the fact that members of the movement are willing to give its basic values primacy in guiding their personal development, regardless of loss or disapproval.

HIPPIE VALUE SYSTEMS

Hippies give absolute allegiance to two values: universal love and the unique value of the individual. Of the Christian religions, Eastern-Orthodox Catholicism is the most collectively oriented and Puritanism the most individualistic.

The Hippie movement, I would suggest, represents a further emphasis on this individualism. For the Puritan ethos the value of the individual in his uniqueness lies in his imitation of Christ, his struggle to act continuously in such a way as to be consistent with the search for the City of Light; but this struggle is hampered, of course, by inner temptations representing the weight of the flesh. In the Puritan ethos there is one strain implying that actions of the elect have an inherent goodness; and then, in its liberal version this becomes the belief that all men are intrinsically good and that with effort, learning, and self-control anyone can succeed in "realizing himself." But whether fundamentalist or liberal, the Puritan ethos is suspicious of pleasure and holds that the direction of the good lies away from gratification of the flesh. The uniqueness of the individual resides in the unpredictable diversity of his struggles with the world and the flesh. An act, to be good, must be a personal effort rather than represent compliance with Church and State. While "nobody can tell you what to do" in any particular situation, the direction is nevertheless clear and common to all men: they must build the City of God on earth.

Though it has roots in the Puritan ethos, the Hippie conception of uniqueness is different. For the Hippie all men are good if only they give way to their nature, as against the pressures of the social structure. Hence, uniqueness will be found in the cultivation of sincerity and spontaneity. Since all individuals are equally valuable and worthy of love, the desires of each merit realization. Nor is there suspicion of pleasure as a guide to action, and of sensual pleasure in particular. But sensual pleasure is seen not so much in its hedonistic light (there is some of this, no doubt) but as a sign of what the individual needs, and a guarantee against domination by others. One must always do what one wants to do; anything else is subordination and loss of independence, *ergo* loss of individuality. Self-expression should know only one limit dictated by the love of others: the other's need for his own self-expression.

THE HIPPIE COMMITMENT TO LOVE

The high valuation of love is in line with all the major religions. In the Hippie movement this is not to remain an abstract dedication to others but must become a warm openness toward all human beings such as precludes competitiveness at any level. In the Western world, at least, men are supposed to love their families and be receptive to outsiders, but they are also supposed to be able to enter into limited relations that are dominated by objectively measured exchanges. Outside the family and friendship, direct expression of the value of love is limited to a willingness to cooperate on the neighborhood or job level, or to a general respect for the rules of the game even if cheating would bring immediate returns. But the Hippie commitment to love goes beyond all this: it implies a permanent willingness to share all of one's possessions with anyone who might require them. It also implies a refusal to judge anyone or to give a person a label like thief, convict, addict, because the code of love requires that the individual always be given another chance—and without expecting anything in return. In fact, love is seen by the Hippies as the normal expression of man unless he is hampered and perverted by social structure. . . .

THE HIPPIE VALUE OF INDEPENDENCE

Another specification in line with the American ethos is the Hippies' high valuation of independence. A man and a woman should be financially and emotionally independent from any other man or woman. This does not preclude developing attachments to particular individuals, but those attachments must involve complete reciprocity and never act as binding obligations upon the other. In order to be valid, a relationship must be totally spontaneous and sincere (there is a tendency to see these two kinds of behavior as synonymous). In the optic of universal love, whether one has a special attachment to someone else is not crucial. What replaces love between man and woman is not hatred or indifference, but simply universal love. If anything, romantic love is under some suspicion, for it tends to withdraw people from the magic circle of universal love. One should not be "hung up" on anything or anybody, one should "keep his cool."

The imperative of "keeping your cool" is strangely in line with the Puritan norm of self-control, although it is certainly not the English version of self-control with its inhibition of aggression and sexual expression. More than a restraint upon self-expression, it is a warning that one should be able to disconnect any relationship that turns out to be upsetting. One should never be so "hung up" on anything, or on any single relationship, that one is led to lose one's temper or feel inordinate grief; one should not allow anyone to possess another human being. Thus, the world can never threaten the Hippie effectively. . . .

MAINTAINING COHESION IN THE HIPPIE CULTURE

Any group whose ideas deviate significantly from the surrounding community has the problem of maintaining solidarity among members whose reason for belonging lies precisely in their social maladjustment. The cohesion and continuity of the group will be furthered if it develops a high ethnocentrism and reduces its relationships to the outside world as much as possible to martyrdom and proselytism [to preach about a cause].

The high ethnocentrism in the Hippie community leads to two consequences. The first is its justification of an exploitative relation to the outside world. Sponging on welfare and petty thievery in record shops, bookstores, university libraries, and supermarkets is accepted because, supposedly, there is a state of war between the square (or "straight") world and the Hippies, a war that is the sole responsibility of the former. Friendly patrons can be used without any commitment on the Hippie's part, since fundamentally they are still the enemy and, after all, they are repaid by the pleasure derived from giving. It encourages a feeling of mutual dependence, the fraternity of the trenches. Merely by belonging to the group, the Hippie gets a feeling of being one of the chosen few. Tolerance is justified because the failings of the chosen are minor in comparison with the importance of being among the chosen. . . .

The tense relationship between the outside world and the Hippie community is maintained by "blowing people's minds," the use of drugs, and work avoidance. "Blowing people's minds" is the obverse of "keeping your cool": its purpose is to shock, disconcert, and thus help disintegrate the "unhealthy" psychological structures of outsiders.

Always permissible against squares [members of straight society], this is supposed to force people to face the futility of their present course of action and make them accept the new wisdom incarnated in the act that "blew their mind." The capacity to blow people's minds has been the only approved way to express aggression, because in its essence it is supposed to be an act of love. Retelling of occasions where "blowing someone's mind" was done successfully against squares is one of the ways prestige is built. And "blowing people's minds" has the advantage of shying clear of police reprisal: it may shock, it may be an act of exquisite cruelty, but it is unlikely to be a legal misdemeanor.

Squares have their minds blown when Hippies offer the spectacle of their decorative spontaneity, in their clothing, hair styles, profanity, public love-making or undressing, gifts of flowers to policemen, sleeping in the streets, in the frenzy and bawdiness of their music, integrated love-making, and self-righteous begging. The "love-in" becomes a sort of Hippie revival meeting. Blowing people's minds is the way to proselytize the world; but it is not an attempt to influence through dialectic, for the choice of the true way must remain one's own. To influence someone is to restrict his freedom. . . .

DRUG USE

A frequent belief among Hippies is that we do not normally use more than 10 percent of our brain power, and that drugs, especially of the LSD variety, permit the expansion of one's consciousness by going beyond the structures of thought derived from role playing and "status games." Thus drug takers are privy to a wisdom that is beyond the grasp of any square, however learned he may be.

Drugs play a major role in cementing the solidarity of the Hippie community. For new members the use of drugs becomes a rite of passage, a way of teaching proper techniques of appreciation. It also serves as a sign of mutual recognition among Hippies and a way to maintain the hostility of the square community.

AVOIDANCE OF EMPLOYMENT

Avoidance of work is equally crucial to the integration of the Hippie community. As the opposite of spontaneity, work is a constraint upon one's fulfillment because it subverts the individual in his uniqueness. Hippies reject the alienation of work because it always requires some and often much self-denial.

Hippies also reject the commitment to exchange that is implicit in work. While the classical Puritan ethos sees in work the idea of service, for the Hippie the impersonality of the market to which work is oriented either directly or implicitly condemns work as a force separating individuals from one another.

The worst form of work is, of course, that which is most common in the modern world, work in the bureaucratic context, which is said to heighten impersonality and subordination and to remove people from nature. The Hippie might try his hand at some craft which puts him into intimate relation with wood, stone, plants—but not with IBM cards and paper clips. To paint, carve, write, or play music is not to work but, on the contrary, to do what one wants, regardless of whether others like the product or not. . . .

THE BENEFITS OF HIPPIE CULTURE TO INDIVIDUALS

The educative impact of the Hippie community has two aspects: first, just by being a member, the Hippie experiences a relief from the self-deprecation that often has characterized these individuals before they joined the movement.

The refusal of career commitments becomes a conformity to the antiwork ideology. Failure becomes a mark of purity: paranoia, the assumed reality of police harassment, passivity kindness. Depersonalization and twilight states can be explained by the use of drugs. Impotence and nymphomania can be seen as expressions of sexual freedom. Homosexual trends can be talked out and even occasionally acted out in festive group occasions without shame and panic.

The tolerance and lack of aggressiveness of the Hippies serve as tranquilizers on many personalities suspicious or anxiety-ridden in their interpersonal relations. The "saints" of the movement often do have a self-confident and benign quality that facilitates their rapport with an "uptight" neophyte. The importance of the group as a shelter, a source of nurturance, and a solvent of guilt facilitates a strong transference for a personality that has gained new self-esteem.

The Hippie collective offers the neophyte the possibility of increasing his rate of interaction with others—and at his own speed. "Keeping your cool" promotes a degree of self-control in personalities where this capacity has often been lacking. A legitimated self learns dissent without fearing exclusion. And then, like the child who discovers his parents are not perfect, the Hippie discovers the discrepancy between the values of the group and the limits of its organization. For eventually he comes to realize that there are freaks and scoundrels as well as saints among the chosen, and that the difference from the square world is perhaps not so great as he first thought. A lasting heterosexual commitment; the subsequent realization that if one wants a good job, it is necessary to complete one's education and/or accept certain bureaucratic disciplines; a growing realization that one is not so young anymore and that the millennium is not for tomorrow—all these can then lead the Hippie to "sell out" and rejoin the meritocracy.

The Anti-Hippie: The Yippie

ABBIE HOFFMAN

In the mid-1960s, as federal, state, and local governments responded more violently to civil rights and antiwar protesters, many student activists broke away from the traditional New Left. The activist groups under this label, such as Students for a Democratic Society (SDS), the Free Speech Movement (FSM), and the Student Nonviolent Coordinating Committee (SNCC), were the first to organize protest against the government's civil rights and free speech policies. In the face of government clampdown, many frustrated activists felt more radical action was called for; some turned to violence and some turned to provocative stunts. In 1966 one of the latter, student activist Abbie Hoffman, created the Yippie Movement, or Youth International Party, to protest both social ills and the increased involvement of American troops in Vietnam. Yippies often used absurd and comic tactics to protest the war in Vietnam, a strategy that they called guerrilla theater. Examples of such protests included a mass demonstration at the Pentagon in which ten thousand people gathered ostensibly to levitate the Pentagon building using powers of the mind, the distribution of thousands of dollar bills on the Wall Street trading floor of the New York Stock Exchange, and the promotion of a pig named Pigasus as a presidential candidate. This excerpt from Hoffman's book *The Best of Abbie Hoffman* explains the strategy of the Yippies and their use of theatrical tactics to garner media attention.

After the 1960s, Hoffman's life was plagued by several drug-related problems. In 1974 he had reconstructive facial surgery and assumed a new identity to avoid arrest on charges of cocaine possession. He eventually came out of hiding and served time in jail.

Throughout the 1980s, he was involved in antinuclear protests as well as several environmental causes. Hoffman also suffered from depression, and on April 12, 1989, he was found dead in his home in an apparent suicide.

A lion walks unnoticed down Wall Street. Slump. Slump. Slump. Strong, determined, with a sense of the future. You are the lion amid the sterile world around you. Where are you going? The lion jumps onto the word *Dreyfus.* *"Growl."* He is satisfied. INVEST IN DREYFUS. Few words are needed. Words confuse. Words are hot. A lion in a street of people is worth a thousand words. It is a wonderful ad, fantastically filmed. A lion walking in a crowded street is totally absorbing. There is an underlying tension of course, but overall coolness. No chaos. No anarchy. No risks. Just give us your dough. Maybe we should run a lion for President?

Projecting cool images is not our goal. We do not wish to project a calm secure future. We are disruption. We are hot. In our ad the lion cracks. Races through the streets. We are cannibals, cowboys, Indians, witches, warlocks. Weird-looking freaks that crawl out of the cracks in America's nightmare. Very visible and, as everyone knows, straight from the white middle-class suburban life. We are a pain in the ass to America because we cannot be explained. Blacks riot because they are oppressed. An Italian cabdriver told me, "If I was black, I'd be pissed, too." America understands the blacks.

A POLICY OF DISRUPTION AND CHAOS

We are alienated. What's that all about? Existential lovers in a plastic society. Our very existence is disruptive. Long hair and freaky clothes are total information. It is not necessary to say we are opposed to the — — — —. Everybody already knows. It is a mistake to tell people what they already know. We alienate people. We involve people. Attract—Repel. We play on the generation gap. Parents shit. They are baffled, confused. They want the cool lion. We tear through the streets. Kids love it. They understand it on an internal level. We are living TV ads, movies. Yippie! There is no program. Program would make our movement sterile. We are living contradictions. I cannot really explain it. I do not even understand it myself.

Blank space, the interrupted statement, the unsolved puzzle, they are all involving. There is a classic experiment in psychology. Subjects are given problems to solve. Some tasks they complete; others are interrupted. Six months later they are given a memory test. They consistently remember the problems that were interrupted. Let's postulate a third setting, in which the subject is shown how to solve the problem by an instructor. It would probably be the least remembered of the three. It is called "going to school" and is the least involving relationship.

When we opened the FREE STORE[1] we circulated a leaflet with a beautiful work of art, and under it in Spanish was the line: *Everything is free at the store of the Diggers.* No address. No store hours. No list of items and services. It was tremendously effective. Puerto Ricans began asking questions. Puerto Ricans talked to hippies. Everybody searched for the FREE STORE together.

WHAT IS "YIPPIE!"?

I stare at a button. Bright pink on purple background: Yippie! It pops right out. It's misspelled. Good. Misspelling can be a creative act. What does Yippie! mean? Energy—excitement—fun—fierceness—exclamation point! Last December [1967] three of us sat in a room discussing plans to bring people to Chicago to make a statement about the Democratic Convention. Hippies are dead. Youth International Party—Y.I.P.—YIP—YIPPIE!. We're all jumping around the room, [activist] Paul Krassner, [activist] Jerry Rubin, and I. Playing Yippie! games. "Y." "Right." That's your symbol. That's our question. "Join the Y." "God, Nixon will attack us in three months for confusing the image of the YMCA." Within fifteen minutes we have created a myth. Head for the media. "Hello, my name is Paul Yippie, what's yours!" Within two weeks every under-

1. a store operated in Haight-Ashbury to provide free supplies to people in need

ground paper has a Yippie! story. In a month *Newsweek* writes "The Yippies Are Coming." Lawrence Lipton, in the L.A. *Free Press*, analyzes Yippie! origins. *Y*'s appear magically on walls around the country. All the while, the excitement and energy are focused on Chicago and people get involved. A Yippie! button produces a question. The wearer must answer. He tells a little story. He mentions Chicago, a festival of music, violence (Americans love to go to accidents and fires), guerrilla theater, Democrats. Each story is told in a different way. There is mass participation in the Yippie! myth. Can we change an H to a Y? Can myths involve people to the extent that they will make the journey to far-off Chicago? Can magic media succeed where organizing has failed? Y not? . . .

TV images flash in my head. Vietnam news pictured in terms of old World War II movies and they are not the Japanese but tiny bands of underdog heroes like beautiful Filipinos I once saw sabotage Japanese Military Might in surprise attack and now nineteen Vietcong guerrillas on heroic mission attack the U.S. Embassy when they said it couldn't be done. Who would have believed that crew-cut generals in shiny limousines and million-dollar planes that zoom by, dropping latest university developments brewed by those institutions we were taught as children to awe, could be whipped by nineteen gooks? America will lose more than its face in Vietnam rice paddies hunting jackknife warriors with napalm machines. Where will be our Alamos? Where even our brave men planting flag on Iwo Jima hilltop? America is a mythic land. Dreamed up by European beatniks, religious fanatics, draft dodgers, assorted hippie kooks, and runaways from servitude off to the New World of milk and honey. Europe said, "If you don't like it here, why don't you leave." Echoed three hundred years later by a middle-aged veteran with sagging ass and sagging belly hunched over sign reading IF YOUR HEART IS NOT IN AMERICA GET YOUR ASS OUT. Sagging crudeness of Joe McCarthy national policy.[2] And even as we slaughtered the Indians, as children we could accept

2. Joseph McCarthy was a senator from Wisconsin who throughout the 1950s accused a number of people of Communist infiltration of the U.S. government.

the encircled group of covered wagons fighting to defend themselves and wanting simply to make it to a little pastureland in the green hills and valleys of California.

The myths of America are strong and good but the institutional machine is a trap of death. Can you believe I was eighteen before I even knew this country had a Depression but at thirteen I could list with correct dates all Revolutionary War battles and discuss in detail the battle of Lexington and Concord which took place just thirty miles from my hometown? *Just last summer I stood on that bridge at 6 A.M. with a follower of Transcendental Meditation and described the battle, joining myself with imaginary musket to the ragged guerrillas that shot from those peaceful hills in Concord on that April morning. The previous day we had stood in Harvard Square passing out free poems hurling curses at the Pentagon gone mad and were attacked by drunk Marines as Harvard fairy professors stood in a circle of [United Nations ambassador] Adlai Stevenson–nothingness and watched and appealed to His Majesty's protectors of law and order, who finally did something. They took down our names and told us to get our asses out of Cambridge. I came away from sitting on the Concord Bridge that night knowing that some day I might just have to shoot a few of His Majesty's gendarmes and forgetting those nights of practicing how to protect my head and nuts in pacifist utero position and believing in the Second American Revolution.* America lost its balls in the frontier and since then there have been no mighty myths and now we hunt for them in lonely balconies, watching *Bonnie and Clyde.* Tragic figures, born out of rejection of a machine-mad American sterility, like James Dean and Marilyn Monroe crushed by plastic Hollywood. And later through a drugged comedian named Lenny [Bruce], who had more balls by far than the stream of district attorneys that chased him with outmoded statutes. . . .

Bah-Bah-Bah-Bah-Bah-Bah-Bah-Bah-Bah Sheep talking rhetoric.

People on the Left spend most of their time telling each other things like that. The point is, everybody already knows, so call it Rhetoric. The Left masturbates continuously because it is essentially rooted in an academic tradition. It is the rhetoric of the Left, its insistence on ideological exactness rather than action, that has held the revolution back in this country as much as the actions of the people in power. The Left has the same smugness as *The New York Times.* I remember about four months ago attending a Mobilization [the Student Mobilization Committee to End the War] meeting as part of Yippie! They did not want to include us in their coalition because they said we had no real constituency. We didn't even request to be included and made a point of asking them not to support us. We just wanted to let people know we would be there. For two days the MOB [Student Mobilization Committee] debated whether or not they should go to Chicago in August [1967]. We laughed at them but not in a hostile way, sort of like Buddhas smiling in the corner. While they argued back and forth we got stoned, made love to all the pretty girls, offered resolutions, like demanding an end to pay toilets and support of the Polish student rebellion (just to upset the Russian-linked U.S. Communist Party), refused to pay for our meals, and in general carried on like bad, crazy niggers. After two days of bullshit they postponed a decision until sometime in July. We came into the hall and passed out huge posters (a picture of the U.S.A. as a jigsaw puzzle all mixed up with an arrow saying Yippie! pointing to Chicago. It said Festival of Life, Chicago, August 25–30—Lights-Theater-Magic-Free-Music). We gave everyone a Yippie! button. All free of course. Then we left, knowing full well they'd all be in Chicago anyway. There was no point meeting with them again and we didn't. . . .

CONFRONTATION IN GRAND CENTRAL STATION

In one week, on fifteen dollars cash, we had attracted five to eight thousand people to a party at midnight, for no reason, in Grand Central Station. It is debatable whether the Grand Central Massacre[3] helped or hurt our chances in Chicago. I main-

3. On March 21, 1968, the Yippies held a "Yip-in" or gathering at New York's Grand Central Station. The police charged the demonstrators and in many cases used violence to try to control the crowd.

tain it helped tremendously. It put Yippie! on the map. I know that sounds cold-blooded. Revolutionists are cold-blooded bastards (the best are also good lovers). I can say this honestly because I run the same, if not more risks, than anyone. I was knocked unconscious by some dumb pig in Grand Central; besides, nobody was under orders to come. (Only people in business really manipulate people because they have money-power and, as everyone knows, money IS power in America.) Besides, I was the only one who tried to cool out the scene. I asked the head cops and the Mayor's assistant, Barry Gottehrer, to let me use the P.A. system. Like dumb cops they refused, in fact they refused even to use it themselves. The Mayor's assistant had an interesting response. "They are not our police," he replied. Asking to use the P.A. system was a very difficult decision which very few people in this country can even begin to comprehend. It means a conscious, deliberate attempt to assert leadership. It's nice in a sense that the cops, as they did later in Chicago, always take over the leadership at such critical moments. "The pigs are our leaders" is the kind of information that is truer than true.

Anyway, a revolutionary artist, which is shorthand for either Revolutionist or Artist, just does it. Life-actors all play their roles according to their backgrounds, talents, costumes, and props. The Grand Central Station Massacre knocked out the hippie image of Chicago and let the whole world know there would be blood on the streets of Chicago. It didn't matter what we predicted, what story we made up, how much we talked of fun and games. The medium is the message and the message was Theater of Cruelty. The rumor of Grand Central Station and the statements of Shoot-to-Kill [Chicago mayor] Daley and Sheriff Joe Woods ("We'll stick them in underground mud tunnels and organize white vigilante groups") were powerful enough magic to separate the hippies from the Yippies.

LSD and the Music Scene

BARNEY HOSKYNS

In 1964 hundreds of people began to take LSD, or "acid," in San Francisco, the center of the hippie universe. By 1965, novice rock performers were organizing giant psychedelic "Acid Tests" where thousands of people would take LSD (which was still legal) and dance to the music of groups such as the Rolling Stones, the Grateful Dead, and Jefferson Airplane. The counterculture scene soon spread beyond San Francisco to many parts of America and the world. In the following excerpt, music writer Barney Hoskyns provides a colorful description of some of the hippies and musicians who took LSD and the music festivals they organized. Hoskyns is an Oxford University graduate who has written several books about music and film, including *Waiting for the Sun: Strange Days, Weird Scenes and the Sound of Los Angeles.* He also has written for *Rolling Stone, Times* (London), *Request*, and *Musician.*

In the summer of 1963, royalties from the acclaimed [novel *One Flew Over the*] *Cuckoo's Nest* . . . paid for a big log house in the hills of La Honda, northwest of Palo Alto. Here [writer] Ken Kesey and his compadres really went for it: Isolated within six acres in a mountain creek, they were free to pursue their [LSD] chemical experiments out of eyesight and earshot, wiring up equipment and speakers in the house and in the redwoods surrounding it so they could groove to [jazz great] Rahsaan Roland Kirk records while chopping wood. Kesey gradually began to abandon writing, seeing it as an essentially reductive and [middle-class] exercise and instead embracing something altogether more primordial and existential.

Everything now came down to the crucial experience of LSD, which made it impossible to continue to live by the straight world's games. When Kesey's tough, larger-than-life pal Ken Babbs returned from active duty as a helicopter pilot in Vietnam, the Merry Pranksters were born, and things became rapidly more intense and maniacal. The Pranksters bought a 1939 International Harvester school bus which had already done service for a family man who'd adapted it for the use of his eleven offspring (with bunks and benches and a sink and so forth), and daubed it with psychedelic swirls and patterns and endowed with intense spiritual significance. The bus was to become a center and a symbol for the Pranksters: You were either on it or off it, cosmically speaking. The Pranksters embarked in the summer of 1964 on an insane, sleepless, paranoid odyssey that took them all the way through the deserts of the Southwest to Texas and New Orleans and then up to New York City for the publication of Kesey's second opus, *Sometimes a Great Notion,* all the while filming their escapades and encounters with straight America. At the rear of the bus hung a sign: CAUTION: WEIRD LOAD; at the front, its destination board read: FURTHUR—with two "u"s. . . .

ACID CHANGED EVERYTHING

Acid changed everything in San Francisco, and the Pranksters were evangelical to the point of zealotry in their attempts to turn people onto it. "Nobody was on any spiritual quest back then," recalled Ellen Harmon, a partner of Chet Helms' in the concert-promotion collective known as the Family Dog. "What it was, was getting away from mother and father so you could do whatever you wanted—which, in most cases, was just lying around and getting as high as you could! Then what happened was, everybody took a bunch of acid and got all *wired*. That's what happened to the scene! They got serious!" Acid was a dividing line between the old and the new, between the old Beat scene and the new youth counterculture. Beat veterans used the pejorative term "hippies"—ironically a term black musicians coined for white beatnik hangers-on in the jazz scene—to describe middle-class kids slumming it in North Beach, but it only betrayed how threatened they felt now that they were no longer running the show. Change was in the air, and the folkies who were in their early twenties knew they had to establish their own scene.

With North Beach becoming expensively gentrified, a number of coffeehouses and hip clothing stores began to open in Haight-Ashbury, a blue-collar, ethnically mixed neighborhood east of Golden Gate Park that was also home to students from the creative hotbed of San Francisco State University. The Blue Unicorn coffeehouse opened in early 1964, and by the summer "hippies" were shedding traditional beatnik garb and wearing the crazier clothes they found in funky [stores]. . . .

The new styles of flowing locks and robes went hand in hand with the new acid consciousness. . . . The Haight's new psychedelic disciples were seeing the world anew, casting off clothes and attitudes that had acted like straitjackets through their repressed adolescences. Life in the Haight took on a zany, freaky, anarchic quality.

MAKING MUSIC ON LSD

Contemporaneous with these mini-revolutions in everyday life was the new sound of electric rock 'n' roll, breaking free of sanctimonious folk protest songs on the one hand and sappy, vapid teenypop on the other. Spearheading rock's revolution were the Beatles, whose hits initially met with scorn on the Bay Area folk circuit but were now making the hippie contingent rethink their stance. With the new wave of British invasion bands taking America by storm, and even Bob Dylan flirting with the ghost of electricity, folkies defected en masse. "The Beatles came along and that was pretty much it," noted Darby Slick of the Great Society. "Folk music just went instantly into the dumper." Slowly, as 1964 turned into 1965, acid began to penetrate pop. By December '65, [the Beatles'] *Rubber Soul* was the Haight's soundtrack. . . .

"One day the idea was there," recalled [Grateful Dead guitarist] Jerry Garcia. "'Why don't we have a big party and you

The Beatles, performing onstage in 1967, are considered by many to be the most influential rock band of all time.

guys bring your instruments and play, and us Pranksters'll set up all our tape recorders and bullshit, and we'll all get stoned?' And that was the first Acid Test . . . right away we dropped completely out of the straight music scene and just played the Tests." Here is the turning point for San Franciscan rock: A band that could theoretically have gone the Top 40/AM Radio/*American Bandstand* route but instead turned away and boldly decided to throw in their lot with a bunch of acid-guzzling renegades in La Honda—renegades, moreover, who by now had been busted for pot and were busily courting the most notorious of all California's subcultural tribes, the Hell's Angels. At a big La Honda party for the Angels on August 7, 1965, the fearsome bikers of Oakland consorted with such guests as Allen Ginsberg—who, as a Jewish New York intellectual homosexual, must have been close to everything an Angel would abominate—and the new acid superdealer Augustus Owsley Stanley III, source of the purest and the best LSD in the world.

Owsley rejoiced in many nicknames—the Bear, the Naughty Chemist, the White Rabbit—and manufactured millions of tabs of LSD. Some say that he kept his prices low, and even gave away as much as he sold. But he could afford to be generous: When LSD was still legal, he was able to buy a 500-gram consignment of the basic constituent of LSD, lysergic acid monohydrate, for $20,000, and turn it into a million-and-a-half doses wholesaling at about $1.50 a piece. In Tom Wolfe's words he was "a cocky little guy, short, with dark hair, dressed like an acid head, the usual boho gear, but with a strange wound-up nasal voice. . . ." At the height of his fame he was thirty years old.

The first "Acid Test," if you could even call it that, took place in a somewhat desultory and disorganized manner at Ken Babbs' house in Santa Cruz, in the fall of 1965. "It started off as a party," wrote Tom Wolfe, "with movies flashed on the walls, and lights, and tapes, and the Pranksters providing the music themselves, not to mention the LSD.". . .

"When it was moving right, you could dig that there was something . . . like ordered chaos," remembered Jerry Garcia. "Everybody would be high and flashing and going through insane changes during which everything would be demolished . . . so there would be this odd interchange going on, electroneural connections of weird sorts." The [Grateful Dead's] decision to become a sort of house band for the Acid Tests . . . was one of the key events in the evolution of the San Francisco scene. Equally important was their decision to attend the second dance staged by Chet Helms' Family Dog collective on October 24. "What this scene needs is us," muttered an acid-flashing [Grateful Dead bass player] Phil Lesh as he wandered amidst the psychedelic throng at the Longshoremen's Hall. . . .

ACID-SPIKED KOOL-AID

[The Family Dog dance at the Longshoremen's Hall] is where it all came together: Where the heads crawled out from the woodwork and discovered each other, where the new hippies realized to their amazement that they actually did constitute a community of sorts and did view the world together through the new lenses of acid consciousness. This is where the soaring folk-rock of the Airplane was heard for the first time outside the [nightclub] Matrix, and where the band's future singer Grace Slick made her first real mark with the Great Society. This is where Ralph Gleason—a forty-eight-year-old, cheroot-smoking, jazz journalist—met a pushy young Berkeley student named Jann Wenner, planting the seed that would become *Rolling Stone* magazine; and where John Cipollina met Gary Duncan and Greg Elmore and talked about founding the [psychedelic rock band] Quicksilver Messenger Service.

The Family Dog threw two further dances that fall: "A Tribute to Sparkle Plenty," headlined by the Lovin' Spoonful, and "A Tribute to Ming the Merciless," headlined by L.A.'s Mothers of Invention. Memorably described on its poster as "a Wham-bang, wide open stoned DANCE flicking on at dusk," "A Tribute to Ming the Merciless" sadly degenerated into a series of ugly brawls—bad vibes all round. Altogether more harmonious was the benefit show for the San Francisco Mime Troupe staged on November 6 by a hyperenergetic Berlin-born Jewish refugee [and future rock promoter] named Bill Graham. . . .

Graham never forgot the sight of the queue stretching along Howard Street on November 6, 1965, waiting to get into the Mime Troupe loft to see the Jefferson Airplane, the Mystery Trend, the Fugs and others play the appeal. He'd had no idea there were so many of these underground groovers out there, primed for multimedia frolics and rock 'n' roll that wasn't just teenage party music. Inside the loft there were films being projected on the walls, and fruit dangled from the ceilings. Booze and acid-spiked Kool-Aid were dispensed from garbage cans lined with aluminum foil. . . .

A PSYCHEDELIC EXPERIENCE

THE ACID TESTS WERE GETTING SERIOUS. The second one, held in San José on December 4, 1965, was flooded with kids who'd spilled out of the Rolling Stones' show that night at the San José Civic Auditorium. Tom Wolfe called it "the first mass acid experience," and *Whole Earth Catalog* founder Steward Brand noted that THERE WAS A DISTINCT "WHIFF OF DANGER" IN THE AIR. No less a personage than Owsley Stanley III showed up for the third Test at Muir Beach Lodge in Marin County on December 18. Ironically, "the Bear" had a bad trip—a hallucinogenic horror-show for which he ever after blamed Ken Kesey.

On January 8, 1966, the Acid Test finally came to San Francisco—to the Fillmore, to be precise. It was the city's first taste of the Pranksters' psychedelic bombardment—what [media critic] Marshall McLuhan termed "sensory overload" and Haight historian Charles Perry called "an overpowering simultaneity." Paramount in the spectacle was a new kind of dancing, relaxed, trippy, flowing with the hypnotic groove of the music and the colors and shapes brought on by the acid. "The Tests were thousands of people, all hopelessly stoned, all finding themselves in a room full of other thousands of people, none of whom they were afraid of," said Jerry Garcia, whose band played the Fillmore that night. Rave culture starts here. In the Fillmore audience was Rock Scully of the Family Dog, who'd been unwise enough to schedule a dance that very same night at the California Hall across town. . . .

The Fillmore Test, broken up by cops at 2:00 A.M. despite the fact that LSD was still perfectly legal, turned out to be merely a prelude to an altogether more ambitious happening dreamed up by *Whole Earth [Catalog]* visionary Steward Brand and artist Ramon Sender, and staged at the Longshoremen's Hall on the weekend of January 20/21, 1966. The Trips Festival, as it was dubbed, was the culmination of the Tests and the Mime Troupe appeals—the ultimate Test, the Test gone truly public. Billed as "a new medium of communication and entertainment, a drugless PSYCHEDELIC EXPERIENCE," it brought together the many strands of the Bay Area revolution: Musicians, dancers, S.F. State students, Berkeley activists, Open Theatre actors, Ron Boise and his Electric Thunder sculptures, and above all the Merry Pranksters, to whom Brand and colleagues offered the Saturday night as an Acid Test. "The general tone of things has moved from the self-conscious Happening to a more JUBILANT occasion where the audience PARTICIPATES because it's more fun to do so than not," the organizers wrote in their announcement. "Maybe this is the ROCK REVOLUTION." It was.

Come the Saturday night, the Pranksters were in their element: Ken Babbs ensconced amidst a huge agglomeration of pipes and platforms in the center of the hall, supervising the many projectors and flashlight machines, Neal Cassady lurching around in a gorilla costume, the fugitive Kesey encased inside an enormous space helmet. Paul Krassner of the *Realist* described what he saw as "a ballroom surrealistically seething with a couple of thousand bodies stoned out of their everlovin' bruces in crazy costumes and obscene makeup." Also wandering around in the midst of the madness was a man who struck Bob Weir of the Dead—and almost everyone else—as "an asshole with a clipboard." It was Bill Graham, who'd been hired to maintain some semblance of order but who was feeling thoroughly freaked out by his first experience of the Pranksters at work.

"Bill didn't have a clue," remembered Owsley. "I realized he was half-terrified by what it was and was doing everything he could to control it and suppress his realization that there was something special going on here." To Graham's disbelief and everyone else's, the Trips Festival made a profit of $16,000: It turned out this hippie shit could actually *pay*. More to the point, it kicked off the brief golden age of San Francisco, before the tourists and the record companies swooped down on the place. In the words of Tom Wolfe, "the Haight-Ashbury era began that weekend."

CHAPTER 3

BLACK POWER AND CIVIL RIGHTS IN THE MID-1960S

AMERICAN
SOCIAL
MOVEMENTS

The Importance of Nonviolent Protest

MARTIN LUTHER KING JR.

In March 1965 civil rights leader Martin Luther King Jr. and members of his Southern Christian Leadership Conference (SCLC) joined a voting rights protest march from Selma, Alabama, to the state capital of Montgomery, a distance of fifty miles. The goal of the march was to draw national attention to the struggle for black voting rights in the state. On Sunday, March 7, police beat and tear-gassed marchers outside Selma and disrupted the march. Television cameras captured the violence and aired it before a national audience. The day came to be known as Bloody Sunday and resulted in an outpouring of public support for the cause.

Following the events of Bloody Sunday, the SCLC petitioned for and received a federal court order barring police from interfering with a renewed march to Montgomery. Two weeks after the Bloody Sunday incident, more than eight thousand people set out toward Montgomery. Five days later they arrived in Montgomery, where King addressed a protest rally of more than twenty thousand people. In his speech King stresses the value of nonviolent protest, even in the face of physical harm at the hands of local and state authorities. He believed that adhering to nonviolence would achieve a central goal of the civil rights movement—equal access to the polls. The protest rallied much support for the Voting Rights Act of 1965, signed into law in August by President Lyndon B. Johnson. The act banned the use of literacy tests and other voter qualification tests that had been used to prevent blacks from registering to vote.

M y dear and abiding friend, Ralph Abernathy, and to all of the distinguished Americans seated here on the ros-

Martin Luther King Jr., address at the Conclusion of the Selma to Montgomery March, Montgomery, Alabama, March 1965. Copyright © 1965 by The Heirs to the Estate of Martin Luther King Jr. Reproduced by permission of the Writers House, Inc.

trum, my friends and coworkers of the state of Alabama, and to all of the freedom-loving people who have assembled here this afternoon from all over our nation and from all over the world: Last Sunday, more than eight thousand of us started on a mighty walk from Selma, Alabama. We have walked through desolate valleys and across the trying hills. We have walked on meandering highways and rested our bodies on rocky byways. Some of our faces are burned from the outpourings of the sweltering sun. Some have literally slept in the mud. We have been drenched by the rain. Our bodies are tired, our feet are somewhat sore.

But today, as I stand before you and think back over that great march, I can say, as Sister Pollard said—a seventy-year-old Negro woman who lived in this community during the bus boycott—and one day, she was asked while walking if she didn't want to ride. And when she answered, "No," the person said, "Well, aren't you tired?" With her ungrammatical profundity, she said, "My feets is tired, but my soul is rested." And in a real sense this afternoon, we can say that our feet are tired, but our souls are rested.

They told us we wouldn't get here. There were those who said that we would get here only over their dead bodies, but all the world today knows that we are here and we are standing before the forces of power in the state of Alabama saying, "We ain't goin' let nobody turn us around."

Now it is not an accident that one of the great marches of American history should terminate in Montgomery, Alabama. Just ten years ago, in this very city, a new philosophy was born of the Negro struggle. Montgomery was the first city in the South in which the entire Negro community united and squarely faced its age-old oppressors. Out of this struggle, more than bus [de]segregation was won; a new idea, more powerful than guns or clubs, was born. Negroes took it and carried it across the South in epic battles that electrified the nation and the world.

Yet, strangely, the climactic conflicts always were fought and won on Alabama soil. After Montgomery's, heroic confrontations loomed up in Mississippi, Arkansas, Georgia, and elsewhere. But not until the colossus of segregation was challenged in Birmingham did the conscience of America begin to bleed. White America was profoundly aroused by Birmingham because it witnessed the whole community of Negroes facing error and brutality with majestic scorn and heroic courage. And from the wells of this democratic sprit, the nation finally forced Congress to write legislation, in the hope that it would eradicate the stain of Birmingham. The Civil Rights Act of 1964 gave Negroes some part of their rightful dignity, but without the vote it was dignity without strength.

Once more the method of nonviolent resistance was unsheathed from its scabbard, and once again an entire community was mobilized to confront the adversary. And again the brutality of a dying order shrieks across the land. Yet Selma, Alabama, became a shining moment in the conscience of man. If the worst in American life lurked in its dark streets, the best of American instincts arose passionately from across the nation to overcome it. . . .

A SHORT HISTORY OF JIM CROW

Our whole campaign in Alabama has been centered around the right to vote. In focusing the attention of the nation and the world today on the flagrant denial of the right to vote, we are exposing the very origin, the root cause, of racial segregation in the Southland. Racial segregation as a way of life did not come about as a natural result of hatred between the races immediately after the Civil War. There were no laws segregating the races then. As the noted historian C. Vann Woodward, in his book *The Strange Career of Jim Crow*, clearly points out, the segregation of the races was really a political stratagem employed by the emerging Bourbon interests in the South to keep the southern masses divided and southern labor the cheapest in the land. You see, it was a simple thing to keep the poor white masses working for near-starvation wages in the years that followed the Civil War. Why, if the poor white plantation or mill worker became dissatisfied with his low wages, the plantation or mill owner would merely threaten to fire him and hire a former Negro slave and pay him even less. Thus, the southern wage level was kept almost unbearably low.

Toward the end of the Reconstruction era, something very significant happened. There developed what was known as the Populist Movement. The leaders of this movement began awakening the poor white masses and the former Negro slaves to the fact that they were being fleeced by the emerging Bourbon interests. Not only that, but they began uniting the Negro and white masses into a voting bloc that threatened to drive the Bourbon interests from the command posts of political power in the South.

REVIVING WHITE SUPREMACY

To meet this threat, the southern aristocracy began immediately to engineer this development of a segregated society. I want you to follow me through here because this is very important to see the roots of racism and the denial of the right to vote. Through their control of mass media, they revised the doctrine of white supremacy. They saturated the thinking of the poor white masses with it, thus clouding their minds to the real issue involved in the Populist Movement. They then directed the placement on the books of the South of laws that made it a crime for Negroes and whites to come together as equals at any level. And that did it. That crippled and eventually destroyed the Populist Movement of the nineteenth century. . . .

If it may be said of the slavery era that the white man took the world and gave the Negro Jesus, then it may be said of the Reconstruction era that the southern aristocracy took the world and gave the poor white man Jim Crow [laws]. He gave him Jim Crow, and when his wrinkled stomach cried out for the food that his empty pockets could not provide, he ate Jim Crow, a psychological bird that told him that no matter how bad off he was, at least he was a white man, better than the black man. And he ate Jim Crow. And when his undernourished children cried out for the necessities that his low wages could not provide, he showed them the Jim Crow signs on the buses and in the stores, on the streets and in the public buildings. And his children, too, learned to feed upon Jim Crow, their last outpost of psychological oblivion.

Thus the threat of the free exercise of the ballot by the Negro and white masses alike resulted in the establishment of a segregated society. They segregated southern money from the poor whites; they segregated southern mores from the rich whites; they segregated southern churches from Christianity; they segregated southern minds from honest thinking; and they segregated the Negro from everything. That's what happened when the Negro and white masses of the South threatened to unite and build a great society: a society of justice where none would prey upon the weakness of others, a society of plenty where greed and poverty would be done away, a society of brotherhood where every man would respect the dignity and worth of human personality. . . .

MOVING AGAINST THE TIDE OF RACISM

Today I want to tell the city of Selma, today I want to say to the state of Alabama, today I want to say to the people of America and the nations of the world, that we are not about to turn around. We are on the move now.

Yes, we are on the move and no wave of racism can stop us. We are on the move now. The burning of our churches will not deter us. The bombing of our homes will not dissuade us. We are on the move now. The beating and killing of our clergymen and young people will not divert us. We are on the move now. The wanton release of their known murderers will not discourage us. We are on the move now. Like an idea whose time has come, not even the marching of mighty armies can halt us. We are moving to the land of freedom.

Let us therefore continue our triumphant march to the realization of the American dream. Let us march on segregated housing until every ghetto of social and economic depression dissolves, and Negroes and whites live side by side in decent, safe, and sanitary housing. Let us march on segregated schools until every vestige of segregated and inferior education be-

Martin Luther King Jr. addresses a crowd of civil rights demonstrators in 1965. King urged his followers to remain calm in the face of adversity.

comes a thing of the past, and Negroes and whites study side by side in the socially healing context of the classroom. . . .

REMEMBERING THE SOLDIERS OF NONVIOLENCE

In the glow of the lamplight on my desk a few nights ago, I gazed again upon the wondrous sign of our times, full of hope and promise of the future. And I smiled to see in the newspaper photographs of many a decade ago, the faces so bright, so solemn, of our valiant heroes, the people of Montgomery. To this list may be added the names of all those who have fought and, yes, died in the nonviolent army of our day: [NAACP activist] Medgar Evers; three civil rights workers in Mississippi last summer; [murdered activist] William Moore; the Reverend

James Reeb[1]; [murdered activist] Jimmy Lee Jackson; and four little girls in the church of God in Birmingham[2] on Sunday morning. In spite of this, we must go on and be sure that they did not die in vain. The pattern of their feet as they walked through Jim Crow barriers in the great stride toward freedom is the thunder of the marching men of Joshua, and the world rocks beneath their tread.

My people, my people, listen. The battle is in our hands. The battle is in our hands in Mississippi and Alabama and all over the United States. I know there is a cry today in Alabama, we see it in numerous editorials: "When will Martin Luther King, SCLC [Southern Christian Leadership Conference], SNCC [Student Nonviolent Coordinating Committee], and all of these civil rights agitators and all of the white clergymen and labor leaders and students and others get out of our community and let Alabama return to normalcy?"

I have a message that I would like to leave with Alabama this evening. That is exactly what we don't want, and we will not allow it to happen, for we know that it was normalcy in Marion that led to the brutal murder of Jimmy Lee Jackson. It was normalcy in Birmingham that led to the murder on Sunday morning of four beautiful, unoffending, innocent girls. It was normalcy on Highway 80 that led state troopers to use tear gas and horses and billy clubs against unarmed human beings who were simply marching for justice. It was normalcy by a café in Selma, Alabama, that led to the brutal beating of Reverend James Reeb.

It is normalcy all over our country which leaves the Negro perishing on a lonely island of poverty in the midst of a vast ocean of material prosperity. It is normalcy all over Alabama that prevents the Negro from becoming a registered voter. No, we will not allow Alabama to return to normalcy.

The only normalcy that we will settle for is the normalcy that recognizes the dignity and worth of all of God's children.

---

1. a white clergyman from Boston who was killed in Selma   2. On September 15, 1963, four young black girls were killed when the Sixteenth Street Baptist Church was bombed.

The only normalcy that we will settle for is the normalcy that allows judgment to run down like waters, and righteousness like a mighty stream. The only normalcy that we will settle for is the normalcy of brotherhood, the normalcy of true peace, the normalcy of justice.

A CONTINUED COMMITMENT TO NONVIOLENCE

And so as we go away this afternoon, let us go away more than ever before committed to this struggle and committed to nonviolence. I must admit to you there are still some difficult days ahead. We are still in for a season of suffering in many of the black belt counties of Alabama, many areas of Mississippi, many areas of Louisiana. I must admit to you there are still jail cells waiting for us, and dark and difficult moments. If we will go on with the faith that nonviolence and its power can transform dark yesterdays into bright tomorrows, we will be able to change all of these conditions.

And so I plead with you this afternoon as we go ahead: remain committed to nonviolence. Our aim must never be to defeat or humiliate the white man, but to win his friendship and understand. We must come to see that the end we seek is a society at peace with itself, a society that can live with its conscience. And that will be a day not of the white man, not of the black man. That will be the day of man as man.

The New Black Revolutionary

MALCOLM X

Malcolm X was one of the primary proponents of violent opposition to white authority in the civil rights movement. From the 1950s until the early 1960s, he served as a leader of the Nation of Islam, a group of black Muslims who advocated segregation of the races and black economic self-sufficiency as the best ways to safeguard the rights of African Americans. In the following speech delivered on April 8, 1964, Malcolm X addresses an audience of the Militant Labor Forum, a group promoting black militancy in the civil rights movement. In this speech, he argues that the African American community must take their constitutional rights by force, if necessary. He also states that the only way to avoid a violent uprising by African Americans is to guarantee them equal access to the vote.

It is important to note that this speech was given before Malcolm X left the Nation of Islam in January 1965. Therefore the views expressed in this speech do not reflect those he held near the end of his life. Prior to 1965, Malcolm X advocated a distinct separation of the races so that African Americans could create their own communities and support their own economic interests. In the months preceding his death, he renounced this belief and focused his efforts on helping blacks achieve the right to vote. He argued that by gaining the power to vote, black communities could elect public officials who would address the needs of African Americans nationwide. However, he did not live to see this goal realized. Malcolm X was assassinated on February 21, 1965, just six months before the passage of the Voting Rights Act of 1965, an act that guaranteed African Americans unhindered access to the polls.

Malcolm X, *Malcolm X Speaks: Selected Speeches and Statements*, edited by George Breitman. New York: Grove Weidenfeld, 1965. Copyright © 1965 by Betty Shabazz and Pathfinder Press. All rights reserved. Reproduced by permission.

F riends and enemies: Tonight I hope that we can have a little fireside chat with as few sparks as possible being tossed
around. Especially because of the very explosive condition that
the world is in today. Sometimes, when a person's house is on
fire and someone comes in yelling fire, instead of the person
who is awakened by the yell being thankful, he makes the mistake of charging the one who awakened him with having set
the fire. I hope that this little conversation tonight about the
black revolution won't cause many of you to accuse us of ig-
niting it when you find it at your doorstep. . . .

During recent years there has been much talk about a population explosion. Whenever they are speaking of the population explosion, in my opinion they are referring primarily to
the people in Asia or in Africa—the black, brown, red, and
yellow people. It is seen by people of the West that, as soon as
the standard of living is raised in Africa and Asia, automatically the people begin to reproduce abundantly. And there has
been a great deal of fear engendered by this in the minds of
the people of the West, who happen to be, on this earth, a very
small minority.

A Western Fear of Minority Growth

In fact, in most of the thinking and planning of whites in the
West today, it's easy to see the fear in their minds, conscious
minds and subconscious minds, that the masses of dark people
in the East, who already outnumber them, will continue to increase and multiply and grow until they eventually overrun the
people of the West like a human sea, a human tide, a human
flood. And the fear of this can be seen in the minds, in the actions, of most of the people here in the West in practically
everything that they do. It governs their political views and it
governs their economic views and it governs most of their attitudes toward the present society.

I was listening to [Everett] Dirksen, the senator from Illinois, in Washington, D.C., filibustering the civil-rights bill; and
one thing that he kept stressing over and over and over was
that if this bill is passed, it will change the social structure of

America. Well, I know what he's getting at, and I think that most other people today, and especially our people, know what is meant when these whites, who filibuster these bills, express fears of changes in the social structure. Our people are beginning to realize what they mean.

THE RACIAL EXPLOSION IN AMERICA

Just as we can see that all over the world one of the main problems facing the West is race, likewise here in America today, most of your Negro leaders as well as the whites agree that 1964 itself appears to be one of the most explosive years yet in the history of America on the racial front, on the racial scene. Not only is this racial explosion probably to take place in America, but all of the ingredients for this racial explosion in America to blossom into a world-wide racial explosion present themselves right here in front of us. America's racial powder keg, in short, can actually fuse or ignite a world-wide powder keg.

There are whites in this country who are still complacent when they see the possibilities of racial strife getting out of hand. You are complacent simply because you think you outnumber the racial minority in this country; what you have to bear in mind is wherein you might outnumber us in this country, you don't outnumber us all over the earth.

Any kind of racial explosion that takes place in this country today, in 1964, is not a racial explosion that can be confined to the shores of America. It is a racial explosion that can ignite the racial powder keg that exists all over the planet that we call earth. I think that nobody would disagree that the dark masses of Africa and Asia and Latin America are already seething with bitterness, animosity, hostility, unrest, and impatience with the racial intolerance that they themselves have experienced at the hands of the white West. . . .

THE BLACK NATIONALIST

The black nationalists to many of you may represent only a minority in the community. And therefore you might have a tendency to classify them as something insignificant. But just as the fuse is the smallest part or the smallest piece in the powder keg, it is yet that little fuse that ignites the entire powder keg. The black nationalists to you may represent a small minority in the so-called Negro community. But they just happen to be composed of the type of ingredient necessary to fuse or ignite the entire black community.

And this is one thing that whites—whether you call yourselves liberals or conservatives or racists or whatever else you might choose to be—one thing that you have to realize is, where the black community is concerned, although the large majority you come in contact with may impress you as being moderate and patient and loving and long-suffering and all that kind of stuff, the minority who you consider to be Muslims or nationalists happen to be made of the type of ingredient that can easily spark the black community. This should be understood. Because to me a powder keg is nothing without a fuse.

1964 will be America's hottest year; her hottest year yet; a year of much racial violence and much racial bloodshed. But it won't be blood that's going to flow only on one side. The new generation of black people that have grown up in this country during recent years are already forming the opinion, and it's just opinion, that if there is to be bleeding, it should be reciprocal—bleeding on both sides.

BLACK NATIONALISM AS A UNIFIED MOVEMENT

It should also be understood that the racial sparks that are ignited here in America today could easily turn into a flaming fire abroad, which means it could engulf all the people of this earth into a giant race war. You cannot confine it to one little neighborhood, or one little community, or one little country. What happens to a black man in America today happens to the black man in Africa. What happens to a black man in America and Africa happens to the black man in Asia and to the man down in Latin America. What happens to one of us today happens to all of us. And when this is realized, I think that the whites—who are intelligent even if they aren't moral or aren't just or aren't impressed by legalities—those who are intelligent will realize that when they touch this one, they are touching all of them, and this in itself will have a tendency to be a checking factor.

The seriousness of this situation must be faced up to. I was in Cleveland last night, Cleveland, Ohio. In fact I was there Friday, Saturday and yesterday. Last Friday the warning was given that this is a year of bloodshed, that the black man has ceased to turn the other cheek, that he has ceased to be non-violent, that he has ceased to feel that he must be confined by all these restraints that are put upon him by white society in struggling for what white society says he was supposed to have had a hundred years ago.

So today, when the black man starts reaching out for what America says are his rights, the black man feels that he is within his rights—when he becomes the victim of brutality by those who are depriving him of his rights—to do whatever is necessary to protect himself. An example of this was taking place last night at this same time in Cleveland, where the police were putting water hoses on our people there and also throwing tear gas at them—and they met a hail of stones, a hail of rocks, a hail of bricks. A couple of weeks ago in Jacksonville, Florida, a young teen-age Negro was throwing Molotov cocktails.

Well, Negroes didn't do this ten years ago. But what you should learn from this is that they are waking up. It was stones yesterday, Molotov cocktails today; it will be hand grenades tomorrow and whatever else is available the next day. The seriousness of this situation must be faced up to. . . .

The American Strategy of Discrimination

There is no system more corrupt than a system that represents itself as the example of freedom, the example of democracy, and can go all over this earth telling other people how to straighten out their house, when you have citizens of this country who have to use bullets if they want to cast a ballot.

The greatest weapon the colonial powers have used in the

past against our people has always been divide-and-conquer. America is a colonial power. She has colonized 22 million Afro-Americans by depriving us of first-class citizenship, by depriving us of civil rights, actually by depriving us of human rights. She has not only deprived us of the right to be a citizen, she has deprived us of the right to be human beings, the right to be recognized and respected as men and women. In this country the black can be fifty years old and he is still a "boy."

I grew up with white people. I was integrated before they even invented the word and I have never met white people yet—if you are around them long enough—who won't refer to you as a "boy" or a "gal," no matter how old you are or what school you came out of, no matter what your intellectual or professional level is. In this society we remain "boys."

So America's strategy is the same strategy as that which was used in the past by the colonial powers: divide and conquer. She plays one Negro leader against the other. She plays one Negro organization against the other. She makes us think we have different objectives, different goals. As soon as one Negro says something, she runs to this Negro and asks him, "What do you think about what he said?" Why, anybody can see through that today—except some of the Negro leaders.

GOALS OF THE BLACK REVOLUTION

All of our people have the same goals, the same objective. That objective is freedom, justice, equality. All of us want recognition and respect as human beings. We don't want to be integrationists. Nor do we want to be separationists. We want to be human beings. Integration is only a method that is used by some groups to obtain freedom, justice, equality and respect as human beings. Separation is only a method that is used by other groups to obtain freedom, justice, equality or human dignity.

Our people have made the mistake of confusing the methods with the objectives. As long as we agree on objectives, we should never fall out with each other just because we believe in different methods or tactics or strategy to reach a common objective.

We have to keep in mind at all times that we are not fighting for integration, nor are we fighting for separation. We are fighting for recognition as human beings. We are fighting for the right to live as free humans in this society. In fact, we are actually fighting for rights that are even greater than civil rights and that is human rights. . . .

MAKING RACISM A HUMAN RIGHTS STRUGGLE

The civil-rights struggle involves the black man taking his case to the white man's court. But when he fights it at the human-rights level, it is a different situation. It opens the door to take Uncle Sam to the world court. The black man doesn't have to go to court to be free. Uncle Sam should be taken to court and made to tell why the black man is not free in a so-called free society. Uncle Sam should be taken into the United Nations and charged with violating the UN charter of human rights.

You can forget civil rights. How are you going to get civil rights with men like [Mississippi senator James] Eastland and men like [Illinois senator Everett] Dirksen and men like [President Lyndon] Johnson? It has to be taken out of their hands and taken into the hands of those whose power and authority exceed theirs. Washington has become too corrupt. Uncle Sam has become bankrupt when it comes to a conscience—it is impossible for Uncle Sam to solve the problem of 22 million black people in this country. It is absolutely impossible to do it in Uncle Sam's courts—whether it is the Supreme Court or any other kind of court that comes under Uncle Sam's jurisdiction.

The only alternative that the black man has in America today is to take it out of Senator Dirksen's and Senator Eastland's and President Johnson's jurisdiction and take it downtown on the East River and place it before that body of men who represent international law, and let them know that the human rights of black people are being violated in a country that professes to be the moral leader of the free world. . . .

So, in my conclusion, in speaking about the black revolution, America today is at a time or in a day or at an hour where she is the first country on this earth that can actually have a bloodless revolution. In the past, revolutions have been bloody. Historically you just don't have a peaceful revolution. Revolutions are bloody, revolutions are violent, revolutions cause bloodshed and death follows in their paths. America is the only country in history in a position to bring about a revolution without violence and bloodshed. But America is not morally equipped to do so.

Why is America in a position to bring about a bloodless revolution? Because the Negro in this country holds the balance of power, and if the Negro in this country were given what the Constitution says he is supposed to have, the added power of the Negro in this country would sweep all of the racists and the segregationists out of office. It would change the entire political structure of the country. It would wipe out the Southern segregationism that now controls America's foreign policy, as well as America's domestic policy.

The Ballot Versus the Bullet

And the only way without bloodshed that this can be brought about is that the black man has to be given full use of the ballot in every one of the fifty states. But if the black man doesn't get the ballot, then you are going to be faced with another man who forgets the ballot and starts using the bullet.

Revolutions are fought to get control of land, to remove the absentee landlord and gain control of the land and the institutions that flow from that land. The black man has been in a very low condition because he has had no control whatsoever over any land. He has been a beggar economically, a beggar politically, a beggar socially, a beggar even when it comes to trying to get some education. The past type of mentality, that was developed in this colonial system among our people, today is being overcome. And as the young ones come up, they know what they want. And as they listen to your beautiful preaching about democracy and all those other flowery words, they know what they're supposed to have.

So you have a people today who not only know what they

want, but also know what they are supposed to have. And they themselves are creating another generation that is coming up that not only will know what it wants and know what it should have, but also will be ready and willing to do whatever is necessary to see that what they should have materializes immediately. Thank you.

Blacks Must Govern Their Own Communities

STOKELY CARMICHAEL

Black Power, a political movement that arose in the mid–1960s, strove to express a new racial consciousness among blacks in the United States. To some African Americans, Black Power represented racial dignity and self-reliance, including freedom from white authority in both economic and political arenas. The movement originated in some ways with Malcolm X, who supplied much of the rhetoric adopted by militant African Americans, but it was Student Nonviolent Coordinating Committee (SNCC) chairman Stokely Carmichael who actually coined the phrase Black Power. Carmichael laid out his ideas of Black Power in a SNCC position paper, titled "What We Want," that first appeared in the *New York Times* on August 5, 1966, and again in his 1967 book *Black Power.* This selection from "What We Want" outlines the need for blacks to end their reliance on white activists and to take greater leadership roles in the SNCC and other civil rights organizations. In line with this position, one of his first major actions as chairman was to reorganize SNCC so that white volunteers would no longer be in positions of leadership.

Carmichael served as SNCC chairman for one year. In 1967 he left on a lecture tour of black communities across the United States. He taught urban blacks to create possibilities for themselves in business and education. In addition, he championed the idea that achieving necessary social change would require blacks to stand together as a powerful and united economic community rather than relying on government welfare programs. In 1968 Carmichael moved to

Stokely Carmichael, "What We Want," *New York Times*, August 5, 1966.

Conakry, Republic of Guinea, in West Africa, where he changed his name to Kwame Ture. For the next twenty-five years, he continued to tour black communities around the world and lecture on the importance of self-reliance within the black community. He died in 1998 due to complications from prostate cancer.

The myth that the Negro is somehow incapable of liberating himself, is lazy, etc., came out of the American experience. In the books that children read, whites are always "good" (good symbols are white), blacks are "evil" or seen as savages in movies, their language is referred to as a "dialect," and black people in this country are supposedly descended from savages.

Any white person who comes into the movement has the concepts in his mind about black people, if only subconsciously. He cannot escape them because the whole society has geared his subconscious in that direction. . . .

REINFORCING NEGATIVE STEREOTYPES

Negroes in this country have never been allowed to organize themselves because of white interference. As a result of this, the stereotype has been reinforced that blacks cannot organize themselves. The white psychology that blacks have to be watched, also reinforces this stereotype. Blacks, in fact, feel intimidated by the presence of whites, because of their knowledge of the power that whites have over their lives. One white person can come into a meeting of black people and change the complexion of that meeting. . . .

If people must express themselves freely, there has to be a climate in which they can do this. If blacks feel intimidated by whites, then they are not liable to vent the rage that they feel about whites in the presence of whites—especially not the black people whom we are trying to organize, i.e., the broad masses of black people. A climate has to be created whereby blacks can express themselves. The reasons that whites must be excluded is not that one is anti-white, but because the effects that one is trying to achieve cannot succeed because whites have an intimidating effect. Ofttimes, the intimidating effect is in direct proportion to the amount of degradation that black people have suffered at the hands of white people.

THE PROBLEM WITH WHITE ACTIVISM

It must be offered that white people who desire change in this country should go where that problem (racism) is most manifest. The problem is not in the black community. The white people should go into white communities where the whites have created power for the express purpose of denying blacks human dignity and self-determination. Whites who come into the black community with ideas of change seem to want to absolve the power structure of its responsibility for what it is doing, and saying that change can only come through black unity, which is the worst kind of paternalism. This is not to say that whites have not had an important role in the movement. In the case of Mississippi, their role was very key in that they helped give blacks the right to organize, but that role is now over, and it should be.

People now have the right to picket, the right to give out leaflets, the right to vote, the right to demonstrate, the right to print.

These things which revolve around the right to organize have been accomplished mainly because of the entrance of white people into Mississippi, in the summer of 1964. Since these goals have now been accomplished, whites' role in the movement has now ended. What does it mean if black people, once having the right to organize, are not allowed to organize themselves? It means that blacks' ideas about inferiority are being reinforced. Shouldn't people be able to organize themselves? Blacks should be given this right. Further, white participation means in the eyes of the black community that whites are the "brains" behind the movement, and that blacks cannot function without whites. This only serves to perpetuate existing attitudes within the existing society, i.e., blacks are "dumb," "unable to take care of business," etc. Whites are "smart," the "brains" behind the whole thing. . . .

How do blacks relate to other blacks as such? How do we react to [black baseball player] Willie Mays as against [white baseball player] Mickey Mantle? What is our response to Mays hitting a home run against Mantel performing the same deed? One has to come to the conclusion that it is because of black participation in baseball. Negroes still identify with the Dodgers because of [the first black baseball player] Jackie Robinson's efforts with the Dodgers. Negroes would instinctively champion all-black teams if they opposed all-white or predominantly white teams. The same principle operates for the movement as it does for baseball: a mystique must be created whereby Negroes can identify with the movement.

Thus an all-black project is needed in order for the people to free themselves. This has to exist from the beginning. This relates to what can be called "coalition politics." There is no doubt in our minds that some whites are just as disgusted with this system as we are. But it is meaningless to talk about coali-

Stokely Carmichael, chairman of the Student Nonviolent Coordinating Committee, addresses a crowd of fourteen thousand in Berkeley, California.

tion if there is no one to align ourselves with, because of the lack of organization in the white communities. There can be no talk of "hooking up" unless black people organize blacks and white people organize whites. If these conditions are met, then perhaps at some later date—and if we are going in the same direction—talks about exchange of personnel, coalition, and other meaningful alliances can be discussed. . . .

If we are to proceed toward true liberation, we must cut ourselves off from white people. We must form our own institutions, credit unions, co-ops, political parties, write our own histories. . . .

THE SOLUTION OF SELF-DETERMINATION

In an attempt to find a solution to our dilemma, we propose that our organization [the Student Nonviolent Coordinating Committee] (SNCC) should be black-staffed, black-controlled, and black-financed. We do not want to fall into a similar dilemma that other civil rights organizations have fallen into. If we continue to rely upon white financial support we will find ourselves entwined in the tentacles of the white power complex that controls this country. It is also important that a black organization (devoid of cultism) be projected to our people so that it can be demonstrated that such organizations are viable.

More and more we see black people in this country being used as a tool of the white liberal establishment. Liberal whites have not begun to address themselves to the real problem of black people in this country—witness their bewilderment, fear, and anxiety when nationalism is mentioned concerning black people. An analysis of the white liberal's reaction to the word "nationalism" alone reveals a very meaningful attitude of whites of an ideological persuasion toward blacks in this country. It means previous solutions to black problems in this country have been made in the interests of those whites dealing with these problems and not in the best interests of black people in the country. Whites can only subvert our true search and struggles for self-determination, self-identification, and liberation in this country. Reevaluation of the white and black roles must *now* take place so that whites no longer designate roles that black people play but rather black people define white people's roles.

Too long have we allowed white people to interpret the importance and meaning of the cultural aspects of our society. We have allowed them to tell us what was good about our Afro-American music, art, and literature. How many black critics do we have on the "jazz" scene? How can a white person who is not part of the black psyche (except in the oppressor's role) interpret the meaning of the blues to us who are manifestations of the song themselves?

It must be pointed out that on whatever level of contact blacks and whites come together, that meeting or confrontation is not on the level of the blacks but always on the level of the whites. This only means that our everyday contact with whites is a reinforcement of the myth of white supremacy. Whites are the ones who must try to raise themselves to our humanistic level. We are not, after all, the ones who are responsible for a genocidal war in Vietnam; we are not the ones who are responsible for neocolonialism in Africa and Latin America; we are not the ones who held a people in animalistic bondage over 400 years. We reject the American dream as defined by white people and must work to construct an American reality defined by Afro-Americans.

CRITICISM OF WHITE RADICALS

One of the criticisms of white militants and radicals is that when we view the masses of white people, we view the overall reality of America; we view the racism, the bigotry, and the distortion of personality, we view man's inhumanity to man; we view in reality 180 million racists. The sensitive white intellectual and radical who is fighting to bring about change is conscious of this fact, but does not have the courage to admit this. When he admits this reality, then he must also admit his involvement because he is a part of the collective white America. It is only to the extent that he recognizes this that he will be able to change this reality.

Another common concern is, how does the white radical view the black community, and how does he view the poor white community, in terms of organizing? So far, we have found that most white radicals have sought to escape the horrible reality of America by going into the black community and attempting to organize black people while neglecting the organization of their own people's racist communities. How can one clean up someone else's yard when one's own yard is untidy? Again we feel that SNCC and the civil rights movement in general is in many aspects similar to the anticolonial situations in the African and Asian countries. We have the whites in the movement corresponding to the white civil servants and missionaries in the colonial countries who have worked with the colonial people for a long period of time and have developed a paternalistic attitude toward them. The reality of the colonial people taking over their own lives and controlling their own destiny must be faced. Having to move aside and letting the natural process of growth and development take place must be faced.

These views should not be equated with outside influence or outside agitation but should be viewed as the natural process of growth and development within a movement; so that the move by the black militants and SNCC in this direction should be viewed as a turn toward self-determination.

CHAPTER 4

THE SEXUAL REVOLUTION OF THE LATE 1960S

AMERICAN
SOCIAL
MOVEMENTS

The Women's Liberation Movement

ALICE ECHOLS

On September 7, 1968, during the annual Miss America Pageant held in Atlantic City, one hundred women gathered to protest the continued debasement of women by the media as nothing but sexual objects. The protest received some media attention and some support, but like other protest movements of the 1960s, the modern women's movement had a long way to go before it would achieve success. In the following selection, feminist author Alice Echols outlines the causes that influenced the women's movement, including the civil rights movement. Echols also discusses the rift that developed between militant feminists who sought to eliminate the concept of gender differences and proponents of women's liberation who fought for equality with men while maintaining a strong sense of femininity. Alice Echols is an authority on feminist theory and the counterculture movement of the 1960s. She received her Ph.D. in history in 1986 from the University of Michigan in Ann Arbor. Her award-winning dissertation, a history of the women's liberation movement of the 1960s and 1970s, was published as *Daring to Be Bad: Radical Feminism in America, 1967–1989*. Echols also wrote several critiques of the feminist antipornography movement that were published in the collections *Powers of Desire* and *Pleasure and Danger*. Her best-known work is the award-winning biography of Janis Joplin *Scars of Sweet Paradise: The Life and Times of Janis Joplin*.

On September 7, 1968, the sixties came to that most apple-pie of American institutions, the Miss America

Alice Echols, *Shaky Ground: The Sixties and Its Aftershocks*. New York: Columbia University Press, 2002. Copyright © 2002 by Alice Echols. All rights reserved. Reproduced by permission of the Columbia University Press, 61 W. 62nd St., New York, NY 10023.

Pageant. One hundred women's liberation activists descended upon Atlantic City to protest the pageant's promotion of physical attractiveness as the primary measure of women's worth. Carrying signs that read, "Miss America Is a Big Falsie," "Miss America Sells It," and "Up Against the Wall, Miss America," they formed a picket line on the boardwalk, sang anti-Miss America songs in three-part harmony, and performed guerrilla theater [the performance of rude acts to gain media attention]. Later that day, they crowned a live sheep Miss America and paraded it on the boardwalk to parody the way the contestants, and, by extension, all women, "are appraised and judged like animals at a county fair." They tried to convince women in the crowd that the tyranny of beauty was but one of the many ways that women's bodies were colonized. By announcing beforehand that they would not speak to male reporters (or to any man for that matter), the demonstrators challenged the sexual division of labor that consigned female reporters to the "soft" stories while reserving for male reporters the coveted "hard" news stories. Newspaper editors who wanted to cover the protest were thus forced to pull their women reporters from the society pages.

The protesters set up a "Freedom Trash Can" and filled it with various "instruments of torture"—high-heeled shoes, bras, girdles, hair curlers, false eyelashes, typing books, and representative copies of *Cosmopolitan, Playboy,* and *Ladies' Home Journal.* They had wanted to burn the contents of the Freedom Trash Can, but they were thwarted by a city ordinance prohibiting bonfires on the boardwalk. However, word had been leaked to the press that the protest would include a symbolic bra-burning, and, as a consequence, reporters were everywhere. Although they burned no bras that day on the boardwalk, the image of the bra-burning, militant feminist remains part of our popular mythology about the women's liberation movement. . . .

In its wit, passion, and irreverence, not to mention its expansive formulation of politics (to include the politics of beauty, no less!), the Miss America protest resembled other sixties demonstrations. Just as women's liberationists used a sheep to make a statement about conventional femininity, so had the Yippies [Youth International Party] a week earlier lampooned the political process by nominating a pig, Pegasus, for the presidency at the Democratic National Convention. Although Atlantic City witnessed none of the violence that had occurred in Chicago, the protest generated plenty of hostility among the six hundred or so onlookers who gathered on the boardwalk. Judging from their response, this new thing, "women's

Miss America contestants pose in Atlantic City in 1947. In 1968 women's liberation activists gathered to protest the pageant's representation of women.

liberation," was about as popular as the antiwar movement. The protesters were jeered, harassed, and called "man-haters" and "commies." One man suggested that "it would be a lot more useful" if the demonstrators threw themselves, and not their bras, girdles, and make-up, into the trash can.

But nothing—not even the verbal abuse they encountered on the boardwalk—could diminish the euphoria women's liberationists felt as they started to mobilize around their own, rather than other people's, oppression. [Feminist author] Ann Snitow speaks for many when she recalls that in contrast to her experience in the larger, male-dominated protest Movement, where she had felt sort of "blank and peripheral," women's liberation was like "an ecstasy of discussion." Precisely because it was about one's own life, there was, she says, "nothing distant about it." [Feminist] Robin Morgan has claimed that the Miss America protest "announced our existence to the world." That is only a slight exaggeration, for as a consequence of the protest, women's liberation achieved the status of a movement both to its participants and to the media; as such, the Miss America demonstration represents an important moment in the history of the sixties.

A Quintessential Movement

Although the women's liberation movement only began to take shape toward the end of the decade, it was a quintessentially sixties movement. It is not just that many early women's liberation activists had prior involvements in other sixties movements, although that was certainly true, as has been ably documented by [feminist historian] Sara Evans. And it is not just that, of all the sixties movements, the women's liberation movement alone carried on and extended into the 1970s that decade's political radicalism and rethinking of fundamental social organization. Although that is true as well. Rather, it is also that the larger, male-dominated protest Movement, despite its considerable sexism, provided much of the intellectual foundation and cultural orientation for the women's liberation movement, many of whose ideas and approaches—especially its concern with revitalizing democratic process and reformulating "politics" to include the personal—were refined and recast versions of those already present in the New Left and the black freedom movement. . . .

CAUSES OF A FEMINIST MOVEMENT

Women's discontent with their place in America in the 1960s was, of course, produced by a broad range of causes. Crucial in reigniting feminist consciousness in the 1960s was the unprecedented number of women (especially married white women) being drawn into the paid labor force, as the service sector of the economy expanded and rising consumer aspirations fueled the desire of many families for a second income. As [Columbia University professor] Alice Kessler-Harris has pointed out, "homes and cars, refrigerators and washing machines, telephones and multiple televisions required higher incomes." So did providing a college education for one's children. These new patterns of consumption were made possible in large part through the emergence of the two-income family as wives increasingly "sought to aid their husbands in the quest for the good life." By 1960, 30.5 percent of all wives worked for wages. Women's growing labor force participation also reflected larger structural shifts in the U.S. economy. Sara Evans has argued that the "reestablishment of labor force segregation following World War II ironically reserved for women a large proportion of the new jobs created in the fifties due to the fact that the fastest growing sector of the economy was no longer industry but services." Women's increasing labor force participation was facilitated as well by the growing number of women graduating from college and the introduction of the birth control pill in 1960.

THE PROPER ROLE FOR WOMEN

Despite the fact that women's "place" was increasingly in the paid work force (or perhaps because of it), ideas about women's proper role in American society were quite conventional throughout the fifties and the early sixties, held there by a resurgent ideology of domesticity—what [feminist author] Betty Friedan coined the "feminine mystique." But, as [feminist theorist] Jane De Hart-Mathews has observed, "the bad fit was there: the unfairness of unequal pay for the same work, the low value placed on jobs women performed, the double burden of housework and wage work." By the mid-sixties at least some American women felt that the contradiction between the realities of paid work and higher education on the one hand, and the still pervasive ideology of domesticity on the other, had become irreconcilable.

THE INFLUENCE OF THE CIVIL RIGHTS MOVEMENT

However, without the presence of other oppositional movements the women's liberation movement might not have developed at all as an organized force for social change. It certainly would have developed along vastly different lines. The climate of protest encouraged women, even those not directly involved in the black movement and the New Left, to question conventional gender arrangements. Moreover, as already noted, many of the women who helped form the women's liberation movement had been involved as well in the male-dominated Movement. If the larger Movement was typically indifferent, or worse, hostile, to women's liberation, it was nonetheless through their experiences in that Movement that the young and predominantly white and middle-class women who initially formed the women's liberation movement became politicized. The relationship between women's liberation and the larger Movement was at its core paradoxical. The Movement was a site of sexism, but it also provided white women a space in which they could develop political skills and self-confidence, a space in which they could violate the injunction against female self-assertion. Most important, it gave them no small part of the intellectual ammunition—the language and the ideas—with which to fight their own oppression.

Sixties radicals struggled to reformulate politics and power. Their struggle confounded many who lived through the sixties as well as those trying to make sense of the period some thirty years later. One of the most striking characteristics of sixties radicals was their ever-expanding opposition to liberalism. Radicals' theoretical disavowal of liberalism developed gradually and in large part in response to liberals' specific defaults—their failure to repudiate the segregationists at the 1964 Democratic National Convention, their lack of vigor in pressing for greater federal intervention in support of civil rights workers, and their readiness (with few exceptions) to support President Lyndon B. Johnson's escalation of the Vietnam War. But initially some radicals had argued that the Movement should acknowledge that liberalism was not monolithic but contained two discernible strands—"corporate" and "humanist" liberalism. For instance, in 1965 Carl Oglesby, an early leader of the Students for a Democratic Society (SDS), contrasted *corporate liberals*, whose identification with the system made them "illiberal liberals," with *humanist liberals*, who he hoped might yet see that "it is this movement with which their own best hopes are most in tune."

A REJECTION OF LIBERALISM

But by 1967 radicals were no longer making the distinction between humanist and corporate liberals that they once had. This represented an important political shift for early new leftists in particular, who once had felt an affinity of sorts with liberalism. Black radicals were the first to decisively reject liberalism, and their move had an enormous impact on white radicals. With the ascendancy of black power many black militants maintained that liberalism was intrinsically paternalistic, and that black liberation required that the struggle be free of white involvement. This was elaborated by white radicals, who soon developed the argument that authentic radicalism involved organizing around one's own oppression rather than becoming involved, as a "liberal" would, in someone else's struggle for freedom. For instance, in 1967 Gregory Calvert, another SDS leader, argued that the "student movement has to develop an image of its own revolution . . . instead of believing that you're a revolutionary because you're related to Fidel's struggle, Stokely's struggle, always someone else's struggle." Black radicals were also the first to conclude that nothing short of revolution—certainly not Johnson's Great Society programs and a few pieces of civil rights legislation—could undo racism. As leftist journalist Andrew Kopkind remembered it, the rhetoric of revolution proved impossible for white new leftists to resist. "With black revolution raging in America and world revolution directed against America, it was hardly possible for white radicals to think themselves anything less than revolutionaries."...

Young radicals often assumed an arrogant stance toward those remnants of the old left that survived the fifties, but they were by the late sixties unambiguously contemptuous of liberals. Women's liberationists shared new leftists' and black radicals' rejection of liberalism, and, as a consequence, they often went to great lengths to distinguish themselves from the liberal feminists of the National Organization for Women (NOW). (In fact, their disillusionment with liberalism was more thorough during the early stages of their movement-building than had been the case for either new leftists or civil rights activists because they had lived through the earlier betrayals around the War and civil rights. Male radicals' frequent denunciations of feminism as "bourgeois" also encouraged women's liberationists to distance themselves from NOW.) NOW had been formed in 1966 to push the federal government to enforce the provisions of the 1964 Civil Rights Act outlawing sex discrimination—a paradigmatic liberal agenda focused on public access and the prohibition of employment discrimination. To women's liberationists, NOW's integrationist, access-oriented approach ignored the racial and class inequalities that were the very foundation of the "mainstream" that the feminists of NOW were dedicated to integrating. In the introduction to the 1970 bestseller she edited, *Sisterhood Is Powerful*, Robin Morgan declared that "NOW is essentially an organization that wants reforms [in the] second-class citizenship of women—and this is where it differs drastically from the rest of the Women's Liberation Movement." In *The Dialectic of Sex* Shulamith Firestone described NOW's political stance as "untenable even in terms of immediate political gains" and deemed it "more a leftover of the old feminism rather than a model of the new." Radical feminist Ti-Grace Atkinson went even further, characterizing many in NOW as only wanting "women to have the same opportunity to be oppressors, too."

THE CONFLICT BETWEEN WOMEN'S LIBERATION AND FEMINISM

Women's liberationists also took issue with liberal feminists' formulation of women's problem as their exclusion from the public sphere. Younger activists argued instead that women's exclusion from public life was inextricable from their subordination in the family, and would persist until this larger problem was addressed. For instance, Firestone claimed the solution to women's oppression wasn't inclusion in the mainstream, but rather the eradication of the biological family, which she argued was the "tapeworm of exploitation."

Of course, younger activists' alienation from NOW was often more than matched by NOW members' annoyance with them. Many liberal feminists were appalled (at least initially) by women's liberationists' politicization of personal life. NOW founder Betty Friedan frequently railed against women's liberationists for waging a "bedroom war" that diverted women from the real struggle of integrating the public sphere.

THE LOFTY GOALS OF LIBERATION

Women's liberationists believed that they had embarked upon a much more ambitious project—the virtual remaking of the world. Nothing short of radically transforming society was sufficient to deal with what they were discovering: that gender inequality was thoroughly embedded in everyday life. As Shulamith Firestone put it, "sex-class is so deep as to be invisible." The pervasiveness of sexism and gender's status as a naturalized category demonstrated to women's liberationists the inadequacy, the shallowness, of NOW's legislative and judicial remedies and the necessity of thoroughgoing social transformation. Thus, whereas liberal feminists talked of ending sex discrimination, women's liberationists called for nothing less than the destruction of patriarchy and capitalism. As defined by feminists, patriarchy, in contrast to sex discrimination, defied reform. For example, [lesbian poet and feminist critic] Adrienne Rich contended: "Patriarchy is the power of the fathers: a familial-social, ideological, political system by force, direct pressure, or through ritual, tradition, law and language, customs, etiquette, education, and the division of labor, determine what part women shall or shall not play, and in which the female is subsumed under the male."

Women's liberationists typically indicted capitalism as well. [Feminist writer] Ellen Willis, for instance, maintained that "the American system consists of two interdependent but distinct parts—the capitalist state, and the patriarchal family." Willis argued that capitalism succeeded in exploiting women as cheap labor and consumers "primarily by taking advantage of women's subordinate position in the family and our historical domination by man."

Central to the revisionary project of the women's liberation movement was the desire to render gender meaningless, to explode it as a significant category. In the movement's view, both masculinity and femininity represented not timeless essences, but rather "patriarchal" constructs. (Of course, even as the movement sought to deconstruct gender, it was, paradoxically, as many have noted, trying to mobilize women precisely on the basis of their gender.) This explains in part the significance abortion rights held for women's liberationists, who believed that until abortion was decriminalized biology would remain women's destiny, thus foreclosing the possibility of women's self-determination.

Indeed, the women's liberation movement made women's bodies the site of political contestation. The "colonized" status of women's bodies became the focus of much movement activism. The discourse of colonization originated in Third World national liberation movements, but in an act of First World appropriation was taken up by black radicals who claimed that African Americans constituted an "internal colony" in the U.S. Radical women trying to persuade the Movement of the legitimacy of their cause soon followed suit by deploying the discourse to expose women's subordinate position in relation to men. This appropriation represented an important move, and one characteristic of radicalism in the *late* sixties.

The Battle over Reproductive Rights

BETTY FRIEDAN

One of the most controversial issues of the modern women's movement, and of modern civil rights, has been the debate over a woman's right to reproductive control. In 1960 the oral contraceptive pill was introduced to the American prescription drug market. The effectiveness of the Pill led many women to expand their sexual activities and increased their determination to have more control over their reproductive choices. Also during the early 1960s, thousands of women who took the drug thalidomide, designed to ease the symptoms of morning sickness in the early stages of pregnancy, sought to abort their fetuses when it was discovered that the drug caused severe birth defects. These developments fueled the controversy between conservatives and religious leaders, who objected to women's increased extramarital sexual activity and viewed abortion as unethical, and supporters of increased reproductive rights for women.

In 1964 feminist author Betty Friedan founded the National Organization for Women (NOW). She viewed the debates over abortion and the Pill as waves in a tide of reproductive rights issues. Her organization encouraged women to challenge government legislation limiting a woman's reproductive alternatives. Although abortion was not legalized until the 1973 *Roe v. Wade* Supreme Court decision, the following speech, given by Betty Friedan in 1969 at the First National Conference for the Repeal of Abortion Laws, urges women to forge ahead to make abortion not only a reproductive but a civil right.

This is the first decent conference that's ever been held on abortion, because this is the first conference in which

Betty Friedan, *It Changed My Life: Writings on the Women's Movement*. New York: Random House, 1976. Copyright © 1976 by Betty Friedan. All rights reserved. Reproduced by permission of Curtis Brown, Ltd.

women's voices are being heard and heard strongly.

We are in a new stage in the sexual revolution in America. We are moving forward again, after many decades of standing still—which has been in effect to move backward. Belatedly, we have come to recognize that there is no freedom, no equality, no full human dignity and personhood possible for women until we demand control over our own bodies.

Only one voice needs to be heard on the question of whether a woman will or will not bear a child, and that is the voice of the woman herself: her own conscience, her own conscious choice. Then, and only then, will women move out of their definition as sex objects to personhood and self-determination. This new stage of consciousness is like that of the black revolution. Blacks are no longer accepting anyone else's definition of what their liberty, equality and identity should be, no matter how paternalistic or beneficent it is, whether from sheriffs with bullwhips or kindly white liberals. The blacks finally have the dignity and the self-respect and the guts to say: we're writing our own names; we are the ones to say what we want and where we're going.

Claiming Control over Women's Bodies

Women are finally saying that, too. We are the ones to say what will happen with our bodies, with our lives. We are finally demanding the voice that has not been accorded us, despite all the paper rights that women are supposed to have in America: all the tokenism, the lip service, the pats on the head, the sexual glamorization. The use of sex to sell everything from detergents to mouthwash, the glorification of breasts and behinds are finally being understood by women for what they are: the ultimately denigrating enshrinement of women as sex objects.

The Reproductive Rights Debate

Yesterday, an obscene thing happened in the City of New York. A Committee of the State Legislature held hearings on the question of abortion. Women like me asked to testify. We were told that testimony was by invitation only. Only *one* woman was invited to testify on the question of abortion in the state of New York—a Catholic nun. The only other voices were those of men. It is obscene that men, whether they be legislators or priests or even benevolent abortion reformers, should be the only ones heard on the question of women's bodies and the reproductive process, on what happens to the people that actually bear the children in this society.

The right of woman to control her reproductive process must be established as a basic, inalienable, civil right, not to be denied or abridged by the state—just as the right of individual and religious conscience is considered an inalienable private right in both American tradition and in the American Constitution.

This is how we must address all questions governing abortion, access to birth control, and contraceptive devices. Don't talk to me about abortion reform. Abortion reform is something dreamed up by men, maybe good-hearted men, but they can only think from their male point of view. For them, women are the passive objects that somehow must be regulated; let them only have abortions for thalidomide, rape, incest. What right have they to say? What right has any man to say to any woman—you must bear this child? What right has any state to say? This is a woman's right, not a technical question needing the sanction of the state, or to be debated in terms of technicalities—they are all irrelevant.

This question can only be confronted in terms of the basic personhood and dignity of woman, which is violated forever if she does not have the right to control her own reproductive process. . . .

CONFRONTING SEXISM IN SOCIETY

Women, even though they're almost too visible as sex objects in this country, are invisible people. As the Negro was the invisible man, so women are the invisible people in America today: women who have a share in the decisions of the mainstream of government, of politics, of the church—who don't just cook the church supper, but preach the sermon; who don't just look up the ZIP codes and address the envelopes, but make the political decisions; who don't just do the housework of industry, but make some of the executive decisions. Women, above all, who say what their own lives and personalities are going to be, and no longer listen to or even permit male experts to define what "feminine" is or isn't.

The essence of the denigration of women is our definition as sex object. To confront our inequality, therefore, we must confront both society's denigration of us in these terms and our own self-denigration as people.

Am I saying that women must be liberated from sex? No. I am saying that sex will only be liberated to be a human dialogue, sex will only cease to be a sniggering, dirty joke and an obsession in this society, when women become active self-determining people, liberated to a creativity beyond motherhood, to a full human creativity.

Am I saying that women must be liberated from motherhood? No. I am saying that motherhood will only be a joyous and responsible human act when women are free to make, with full conscious choice and full human responsibility, the decisions to become mothers. Then, and only then, will they be able to embrace motherhood without conflict, when they will be able to define themselves not just as somebody's mother, not just as servants of children, not just as breeding receptacles, but as people for whom motherhood is a freely chosen part of life, freely celebrated while it lasts, but for whom creativity has many more dimensions, as it has for men.

Then, and only then, will motherhood cease to be a curse and a chain for men and for children. For despite all the lip service paid to motherhood today, all the roses sent on Mother's Day, all the commercials and the hypocritical ladies' magazines' celebration of women in their roles as housewives and mothers, the fact is that all television or night-club comics have to do is go before a microphone and say the words "my wife," and the whole audience erupts into gales of guilty, vicious and obscene laughter.

The hostility between the sexes has never been worse. The

image of women in avant-garde plays, novels and movies, and behind the family situation comedies on television is that mothers are man-devouring, cannibalistic monsters, or else Lolitas, sex objects—and objects not even of heterosexual impulse, but of sadomasochism. That impulse—the punishment of women—is much more of a factor in the abortion question than anybody ever admits.

Motherhood is a bane almost by definition, or at least partly so, as long as women are forced to be mothers—and only mothers—against their will. Like a cancer cell living its life through another cell, women today are forced to live too much through their children and husbands (they are too dependent on them, and therefore are forced to take too much varied resentment, vindictiveness, inexpressable resentment and rage out on their husbands and children).

Perhaps it is the least understood fact of American political life: the enormous buried violence of women in this country today. Like all oppressed people, women have been taking their violence out on their own bodies, in all the maladies with which they plague the M.D.'s and the psychoanalysts. Inadvertently, and in subtle and insidious ways, they have been taking their violence out, too, on their children and on their husbands, and sometimes they're not so subtle.

The battered-child syndrome that we are hearing more and more about from our hospitals is almost always to be found in the instance of unwanted children, and women are doing the battering, as much or more than men. In the case histories of psychologically and physically maimed children, the woman is always the villain, and the reason is our definition of her: not only as passive sex object, but as mother, servant, someone else's mother, someone else's wife.

Am I saying that women have to be liberated from men? That men are the enemy? No. I am saying the *men* will only be truly liberated to love women and to be fully themselves when women are liberated to have a full say in the decisions of their lives and their society.

Until that happens, men are going to bear the guilty burden

of the passive destiny they have forced upon women, the suppressed resentment, the sterility of love when it is not between two fully active, joyous people, but has in it the element of exploitation. And men will not be free to be all they can be as long as they must live up to an image of masculinity that disallows all the tenderness and sensitivity in a man, all that might be considered feminine. . . .

EMERGING FROM A PASSIVE EXISTENCE

This is the real sexual revolution. Not the cheap headlines in the papers about at what age boys and girls go to bed with each other and whether they do it with or without the benefit of marriage. That's the least of it. The real sexual revolution is the emergence of women from passivity, from the point where they are the easiest victims for all the seductions, the waste, the worshiping of false gods in our affluent society, to full self-determination and full dignity. And it is the emergence of men from the stage where they are inadvertent brutes and masters to sensitive, complete humanity.

This revolution cannot happen without radical changes in the family as we know it today; in our concepts of marriage and love, in our architecture, our cities, our theology, our politics, our art. Not that women are special. Not that women are superior. But these expressions of human creativity are bound to be infinitely more various and enriching when women and men are allowed to relate to each other beyond the strict confines of the *Ladies' Home Journal's* definition of the Mamma and Papa marriage.

If we are finally allowed to become full people, not only will children be born and brought up with more love and responsibility than today, but we will break out of the confines of that sterile little suburban family to relate to each other in terms of all of the possible dimensions of our personalities—male and female, as comrades, as colleagues, as friends, as lovers. And without so much hate and jealousy and buried resentment and hypocrisies, there will be a whole new sense of love that will make what we call love on Valentine's Day look very pallid.

THE QUESTION OF ABORTION

It's crucial, therefore, that we see this question of abortion as more than a quantitative move, more than a politically expedient move. Abortion repeal is not a question of political expediency. It is part of something greater. It is historic that we are addressing ourselves this weekend to perhaps the first national confrontation of women and men. Women's voices are finally being heard aloud, saying it the way it is about the question of abortion both in its most basic sense of morality and in its new political sense as part of the unfinished revolution of sexual equality.

In this confrontation, we are making an important milestone in this marvelous revolution that began long before any of us here were born and which still has a long way to go. As the pioneers from Mary Wollstonecraft[1] to [family planning activist] Margaret Sanger gave us the consciousness that brought us from our several directions here, so we here, in changing the very terms of the debate on abortion to assert woman's right to choose, and to define the terms of our lives ourselves, move women further to full human dignity. Today, we moved history forward.

1. author of *Vindication of the Rights of Woman*

The Birth Control Pill and the Sexual Revolution

ANN MARIE CUNNINGHAM

In 1960 the Food and Drug Administration approved the birth control pill. By 1970 an estimated 8 to 10 million American women were using the pill, a combination of estrogen and progestin that prevents ovulation. In the following selection, originally written for *Ladies' Home Journal*, freelance writer Ann Marie Cunningham describes the sexual revolution brought about by the introduction of the birth control pill. For the first time, women had control of their reproductive systems and could have intercourse more frequently with little fear of an unwanted pregnancy.

This sense of being in charge of their own bodies also led many women to question the authority of their husbands, doctors, and churches. The sexual revolution did bring some negative consequences. Increasing numbers of men expected women to have casual affairs and one-night stands without any expectation of marriage. Many women, on the other hand, found such no-strings sex left them feeling empty and devalued. However, all in all the pill did provide a previously unimagined degree of freedom and fostered a new and healthy assertiveness among women.

I n June 1960, the oral contraceptive was approved for sale—and transformed our lives like nothing before or since. The Pill, we called it, and everyone from teenage boys to country singers to eminent theologians knew just what we meant. In this age of AIDS, when the very idea of sexual revolution seems both archaic and dangerous, it's easy to forget how truly liberating the Pill seemed to be in 1960. Nothing else in the twentieth century—perhaps not even winning the right to vote—made such an immediate difference in women's lives. Overnight, the Pill gave women control of their reproductive systems; no longer was biology our absolute destiny.

Used properly, this contraceptive was virtually 100 percent effective, and it provoked profound social change. The Pill helped lower the birth rate and end America's baby boom in 1964. It spurred sexual frankness and experimentation. It allowed women to think seriously about careers because they could postpone childbirth. And it sparked the feminist and pro-choice movements; once women felt they were in charge of their own bodies, they began to question the authority of their husbands, their bosses, their doctors and their churches. As Founding Feminist Betty Friedan says today [in 1990]: "In the mysterious way of history, there was this convergence of technology that occurred just as women were ready to explode into personhood." Yet for many women, the Pill turned out to have a decidedly bitter aftertaste. The early versions were at best inconvenient and at worst dangerous, with alleged side effects ranging from dampened libido, depression and weight gain to blood clots, strokes and cancer.

Today's Pill is far safer, and 10.7 million American women now use it. It continues to be the nation's number-one method of birth control. But the profile of the Pill user has altered: Those now most likely to take it are aged fifteen to twenty-four.

Many of these young women, like their sixties' moms before them, regard taking the Pill as a rite of passage. "Most of my friends start the Pill when they begin going steady; it's part of a commitment you make," says Elizabeth, a twenty-two-year-old book editor from New York.

Some of the women who once shared that feeling now express a deep ambivalence, however. The Pill allowed Boomers to postpone childbearing for a long time—in some cases until they were too old to conceive. "I think maybe the Pill made us think we could turn our fertility on and off," says Jan, thirty-five, a college administrator from New Orleans who started taking the Pill as a teenager and decades later found herself unable to have a baby.

There are many other second thoughts about the Pill. Some women wonder if it didn't really do more for men, who availed themselves of the increased sexual opportunities while expecting women to automatically assume the responsibility for contraception. Says University of Washington sociologist Pepper Schwartz, "Since the Pill, men tend to assume that women will take care of protection."

THE INTRODUCTION OF THE PILL

The Pill was developed by a team of Massachusetts-based researchers, including a Catholic physician, John Rock. Its biggest proponent was Margaret Sanger, the founder of the Planned Parenthood Federation of America. "No woman can call herself free who does not own and control her own body," she declared. Produced by the G.D. Searle pharmaceutical company and called Enovid, the original Pill combined synthetic forms of the hormones estrogen and progestin to suppress ovulation.

By 1965, six other companies were marketing their own brands of oral contraceptives. And by the end of the decade, nearly ten million women were taking the Pill, making it America's contraceptive of choice. But almost with its introduction, reports of serious problems began to surface, including blood clotting, heart disease, depression and strokes. After Congress held a hearing on the Pill's health effects, the Food and Drug Administration (FDA) forced manufacturers to include a package insert warning users of all possible side effects. Women heeded the caveats, and during the seventies usage dropped by 20 percent. Consumption recovered to present levels in the eighties, with the development of formulas containing as little as one fifth the estrogen and one twenty-fifth the progestin.

WOMEN FIND NEW FREEDOM

The Pill's greatest effect may have been that it not only kept women from getting pregnant, it helped them change their sex lives. Finally, they could enjoy lovemaking wholeheartedly, without dreading the consequences. Says author Erica Jong, whose 1974 novel *Fear of Flying* was a textbook of sexual liberation, "Because women could control their fertility, they could start thinking of sexual pleasure instead of just pregnancy."

Most experts agree that the Pill contributed mightily to the sexual revolution. Effective forms of birth control—notably condoms—were already available, and sexual mores had begun to change in the postwar era. But the Pill made it easier for women to engage in sex more frequently. One 1965 study of married women who used oral contraceptives found that they had sex up to 39 percent more often than women using other methods of contraception.

And it encouraged public discussion of sex as well. For the first time, women's magazines could talk to their readers about sexual fulfillment, even headlining the word "orgasm" on their covers. Recalls Malcolm Potts, M.D., president of Family Health International, a nonprofit contraceptive-research organization, "You wouldn't mention condoms at cocktail parties, but you could talk about the Pill." And wisecracks about single women who were "on the Pill" were a shorthand for women who had stopped worrying about their reputations and started enjoying sex, just like men.

THE DRAWBACKS OF THE PILL

Here, too, however, the Pill brought mixed blessings. No longer were women looked on as fragile beings to be protected because they were vulnerable to pregnancy; instead they came to be regarded as independent equals who could—and should—take care of themselves. Gone were differentiations between "good girls" whom men would marry, and "bad girls" with whom they'd play around. "Before the Pill," says William Simon, Ph.D., professor of sociology at the University of Houston, "a woman who came prepared for contraception was making a statement about being prepared for sex which moved her to the slut end of the spectrum. The invisibility of the Pill muted that considerably." By the time the sexual revolution was at its height, many men expected women to have casual affairs and even one-night stands. "The key was that this was done without any expectation that it would end in marriage," says John Money, Ph.D., professor emeritus of medical psychology at Johns Hopkins University and Hospital, in Baltimore.

But while some female sexual behavior changed, attitudes did not always keep pace: Many women still wanted emotional as well as physical fulfillment. "One of the characteristics of women that remained true throughout all this was their inability to become sexually aroused without becoming emotionally attracted," says William Simon. "Men can go to bed with someone they don't necessarily like. That was never true of women." For the multitudes of women who did engage in no-strings sex, it soon became an empty exercise.

Nowadays, while we may take a certain degree of sexual frankness and freedom for granted, the excesses of the sixties seem emotionally empty and downright dangerous: We're haunted by AIDS, not to mention more than thirty other sexually transmitted diseases—against which the Pill is useless. . . . Says Helen Singer Kaplan, Ph.D., a specialist in sexual disorders, "The Pill freed young men and women to have sex, but . . . the new fears are forcing them to learn to communicate, to put more energy into making their relationships work instead of seeking out more partners."

WOMEN QUESTION TRADITION

One change wrought by the Pill is still with us today: It raised women's expectations of their lives, and they soon were unwilling to bear a child if the pregnancy was accidental. "Having a baby when you didn't want a baby became unthinkable," says Rosalind Pollack Petchesky, professor of women's studies at Hunter College, in New York City. This attitude, Petchesky says, "undoubtedly contributed to the rise in abortions for women who did not use the Pill and sometimes for those who did."

For some women, the Pill's ramifications went beyond pregnancy and sex. Its reliability encouraged Catholic women to ignore the church's centuries-old prohibition against artificial birth control. Today, between 80 and 85 percent of Catholic women in the U.S. approve of the use of some form of contraception. For most U.S. Catholic women, using the Pill was their first significant rebellion against the church, and it meant that their attitude toward its teachings on other matters would never be quite the same. Says Rev. Andrew Greeley, the sociologist and author, "It has prompted them to question the church. They now make their own decisions on ethical and religious matters when they think the official church is wrong."

In some ways, the Pill has had as great an effect in the office as in the bedroom. In the early sixties, increasingly, numbers of women had already begun trickling into the job market. Their opportunities expanded just as the cost of living exploded, making it both more possible and essential for women to work. The Pill abetted these forces by allowing women for the first time to plan how they would mesh their new opportunities with their reproductive lives. As they did so, the birth rate fell until 1976, when Baby Boomers decided to conceive, creating the baby boomlet. Between 1970 and 1987, the rate of first births among women in their thirties more than doubled, according to the National Center for Health Statistics. For those aged forty to forty-four, it increased 75 percent.

If the Pill helped keep women in the office longer, it also may have made it easier for them to walk out of unsuccessful marriages. "The major influence on a woman's decision to leave her husband is probably whether she can find a job and support her family," says Pepper Schwartz. "But she is more likely to be able to leave if she has two children, not four.". . .

TEENAGE PREGNANCIES

Some parents and religious commentators worry that the Pill has encouraged adolescent promiscuity and teenage pregnancies. It's true that the rate of adolescent pregnancies in the United States, currently stable, remains the highest in the Western world. But a more likely culprit is lack of the Pill and of

information about contraceptives. In 1988, the Alan Gutt-
macher Institute, the reproductive-health research organization
in New York, found that U.S. women, especially teenagers,
take the Pill less frequently than do women of other nation-
alities. One major reason: In the 1980s, state and federal cuts
in social services severely limited teens' access to birth control
and sex education. "We suffer from incredible ignorance about
sexual matters in this country," says Louise Tyrer, M.D., vice-
president of medical affairs for the Planned Parenthood Federation of America.

MALE CONTRACEPTION

In some ways, the Pill's very effectiveness has been unfortu-
nate; American medical researchers have made little subsequent
effort to develop a male contraceptive. But researchers have
lagged on finding better birth-control methods for women as
well. Today, this contraceptive gap is crucial, because the Pill
cannot defend women against AIDS and sexually transmitted
diseases that were no particular threat when it was invented.
Says Susan C.M. Scrimshaw, Ph.D., professor of anthropology
and public health at the University of California at Los Angeles, "In some cultures where AIDS is raging, women find it
next to impossible to enlist their partners in using barrier
methods." She calls on the drug industry to develop an entivi-
ral spermicide that women could use without their partners'
permission. "In a way," she adds, "it's appalling that after thirty
years, the Pill is the best we have."

For all its shortcomings, however, the Pill brought the aver-
age American woman a degree of freedom that had previously
been unimaginable. Given that freedom, women began to look
more thoughtfully at sex, work, marriage, motherhood—and
themselves. Even the Pill's considerable drawbacks prompted
a new assertiveness: Women are now more willing to question
their doctors and their drug companies. As a method of contraception, the Pill [may soon be surpassed by newer tech-
nologies], but the power it conferred on women remains considerable, and its legacy enduring.

Ending Gender Discrimination in the Workplace

RAYMOND MUNTS AND DAVID C. RICE

Before the passage of the Civil Rights Act of 1964, women were not legally protected from discrimination in the workplace. Many employers assumed that women were not physically or mentally capable of performing certain jobs, so women were often excluded from certain fields of employment. This is not to say that legislators had never considered reform. Beginning in 1900, several laws were passed that protected women from the long hours and low wages that accompanied waves of urban industrialization. Regardless of the types of protections guaranteed under the law, it was evident by 1960 that women still fell markedly behind their male counterparts in all areas of employment, especially in wages and education.

Title VII of the Civil Rights Act of 1964 prohibited employers from discriminating on the basis of race, color, religion, sex, or national origin. It is important to note that many states already had laws prohibiting sex discrimination in employment, but Title VII made gender discrimination illegal on the federal level. In this selection, Raymond Munts, a former assistant director of the Institute for Research on Poverty, and David C. Rice, an attorney specializing in employment litigation, examine the history of women in the workplace and the development of the Title VII section of the 1964 Civil Rights Act.

D uring the reform period of the decade preceding World War I, states began enacting protective laws for workers. This was acclaimed widely as a public victory over unchecked

Raymond Munts and David C. Rice, "Women Workers: Protection or Equality?" *Industrial and Labor Relations Review*, vol. 24, October 1970. Copyright © 1970 by Cornell University. All rights reserved. Reproduced by permission.

industrialization. Some of these laws apply only to women, regulating their hours of work and conditions of employment. Now legislatures and courts are taking a new look at women's protective law at the urging of those who fear such legislation restricts women access to certain jobs and places women at a disadvantage in competing with men. The Equal Employment Opportunities Commission claims that Title VII of the Civil Rights Act of 1964 invalidates women's protective law because it prohibits employment discrimination based on sex. This amendment was added to the Civil Rights Act during congressional debate and was regarded, at the time, as a mere maneuver intended to block passage of the Act, but the ultimate fate of female protective law may turn on the primacy of this federal statute.

A Short Overview of Protective Laws

With the rapid growth of industry, finance, and commerce at the end of the nineteenth century, women entered the labor force in substantial numbers. By 1900 the five million female employees constituted 18 percent of the labor force. Public attention was directed by the National Consumers' League and others to the long hours, low wages, and miserable conditions of many working women. Immigration and rapid urbanization had provided an overabundance of female "help." With few skills, low mobility, and no union protection, women were easily exploited. In the reform movement which began about 1900 as a response to unchecked industrial expansion, legislative protection for women and children laborers was a prominent theme.

The reformers argued vigorously for laws limiting the hours of employment for women. By 1913, twenty-seven states had created maximum weekly or daily hours to protect the "health and morals" of women. The constitutionality of using state police power in this way was upheld in *Muller* v. *Oregon* (1908), the case in which Louis Brandeis as counsel for the State of Oregon first introduced the "sociological brief." He built his case almost entirely on the testimony of doctors, sociologists, and economists. Judge Brewer, speaking for the court, acknowledged the "abundant testimony of the medical fraternity" and added,

> History discloses the fact that woman has always depended upon man. . . . Though limitations upon personal and contractual rights be removed by legislation, there is that in her disposition and habits of life which will operate against a full assertion of those rights. She will still be where some legislation to protect her seems necessary to secure a real equality of right: . . . Differentiated by these matters from the other sex, she is properly placed in a class by herself, and legislation designed for her protection may be sustained . . . her physical structure and a proper discharge of her maternal functions—having in view not merely her own health, but the well-being of the race—justify legislation to protect her from the greed as well as the passion of man.

. . . The Muller decision proceeded upon the theory that the difference between the sexes may justify a different rule respecting hours in the case of women than in the case of men. . . . In view of the great—not to say revolutionary—changes which have taken place since that utterance, in the contractual, political, and civil status of women, culminating in the 19th Amendment, it is not unreasonable to say that these differences have now come almost, if not quite, to the vanishing point . . . *we cannot accept the doctrine that women of mature age*, sui juris, *require or may be subjected to restrictions upon their liberty of contract which could not be imposed in the case of men under similar circumstances.* To do so would be to ignore all the implications to be drawn from the present-day trend of legislation, as well as that of common thought and usage, by which woman is accorded emancipation from the old doctrine that she must be given special protection or be subjected to special restraint in her contractual and civil relationships.

FIXING MINIMUM WAGES FOR WOMEN

Thus began a period of fifteen years of ambivalence in public policy with one set of legal precedents supporting state law limiting women's hours, and another group denying women minimum wages. The ambivalence was resolved with the crucial one-vote shift on the Supreme Court which followed the 1936 election and the Court "packing" fight. The case involved a hotel chambermaid, Elsie Parrish, who sued for pay due under a hitherto unenforced Washington state minimum-wage law. The argument of the court was an echo of the argument in *Muller* v. *Oregon:* "What can be closer," said Chief Justice Hughes, "to the public interest than the health of women and their protection from unscrupulous and over-reaching employers? . . . how can it be said that the requirement of the payment of a minimum wage fairly fixed in order to meet the very necessities of existence is not an admissible means to that end?" *Adkins* v. *Children's Hospital* was overthrown, and protection of women's wages took its place alongside protection of their hours. As a result of the Parrish decision and the subsequent enactment of the Fair Labor Standards Act, many states adopted minimum-wage laws. . . .

THE INCLUSION OF WOMEN IN CIVIL RIGHTS

The sixty-year tradition of protective laws for women is being challenged by Title VII of the Civil Rights Act of 1964. The Civil Rights bill was introduced in the House of Representatives without any mention of "sex." While the bill was before the House Judiciary Committee, Howard Smith of Virginia decided to add an amendment which would assure its defeat—equal rights for women. His strategy backfired—both the amendment and the bill passed—and the law became effective July 2, 1965. It is interesting that no women's group petitioned for or supported the sex amendment to Title VII.

A HISTORY OF EQUAL RIGHTS FAILURE

The trivial circumstances leading to enactment of the sex provision of Title VII and the profound changes it eventually may bring appear to qualify as historical accident. Such a conclusion, however, would overlook a tradition of "equal rights" which has long been a counterpoint to the prevailing protectionist policy. Every year since 1923 an "Equal Rights Amendment" has been proposed to the federal Constitution. This amendment covers the ground of Title VII but goes beyond, providing that "Equality of rights under law shall not be denied or abridged by the United States or by any state on account of sex." Its proponents have argued that economic progress has made protective legislation for women obsolete and that the real effect of such law now is to disadvantage women by providing a basis for discrimination under the guise of safety and welfare legislation.

Although the amendment has not been enacted, interest has continued, and in 1961 a Presidential Commission on the Status of Women further investigated these questions. The Commission recommended that minimum-wage and working standards be extended to men as well as women and emphasized premium overtime pay as the way of limiting hours. Until universally applicable standards could come into being, the Commission urged retention of present laws. It also asked for greater flexibility in regard to weight-lifting restrictions, night work, and occupational limitations.

CHAPTER 5

VIOLENCE AND THE ANTIWAR MOVEMENT OF THE LATE 1960s

AMERICAN
SOCIAL
MOVEMENTS

The Chicago Eight Conspiracy Trial

PAUL GLUSMAN

The summer of 1968 was a turbulent one in the city of Chicago. During the Democratic National Convention, held in August, several thousand students gathered to protest U.S. involvement in the Vietnam War. The city's mayor, Richard Daly, ordered Chicago police to actively engage student protesters, an action that started a riot involving fifteen thousand demonstrators and police. Daly felt that his use of police violence was in line with upholding the newly established Anti-Riot Act of 1967. Congress established this law to quell the growing student movement protesting President Lyndon Johnson's Vietnam War policies.

On March 29, 1969, activists Rennie Davis, David Dellinger, John Froines, Tom Hayden, Abbie Hoffman, Jerry Rubin, Bobby Seale, and Lee Weiner were indicted for crossing state lines with the intent to incite violence. These young men became known as the Chicago Eight. The indictment was based on their organization of student protests at the Democratic Convention. They were tried in the court of Judge Julius Hoffman, who was criticized for his bias against the defendants. As a federal judge, Hoffman himself selected the jury members, the great majority of whom were white conservatives. Hoffman dismissed the defense's attempts to remove jurors who might be biased against the defendants. He also made it difficult for the defense team to cross-examine witnesses.

In the following article, social critic and student activist Paul Glusman discusses the trial and the obvious biases of the court. One of the original eight defendants, Black Panther Party leader Bobby Seale, was harshly mistreated during his separate trial and summarily sentenced to four years in prison for contempt of court. In the end the jury acquitted the remaining Chicago Seven on the charge of conspiracy to start a riot, but they found all but Froines and Weiner guilty of attempting to cross state lines to start a riot. Hoffman sentenced each of the five remaining defendants to five years' imprisonment, along with a $5,000 fine, for contempt of court due to their behavior during the trial. On November 21, 1972, the Seventh Circuit Court of Appeals reversed all convictions, basing its decision on Hoffman's biases in selecting the jury and of his deprecatory and often antagonistic attitude toward the defense. At the time this article was written, Glusman was an activist at U.C. Berkeley. His own "conspiracy to incite a riot" trial, known as the trial of the Berkeley Three, had just ended in a hung jury decision.

Judge Julius Jennings Hoffman does look like Mr. Magoo [a cartoon character]. He even talks like Magoo. The first few minutes spent in his pretentious, modern courtroom on the twenty-third floor of the Chicago Federal Building make the whole Conspiracy trial seem absurdly funny.

The diminutive Hoffman is a cranky old man with a high-pitched voice that cracks in the upper registers. His wizened face has led Illinois Black Panther leader Fred Hampton to quip that the judge has so many lines on his head "that he can screw his hat on."

With his eccentricities and his comic-book face, Julius Hoffman is hard to take seriously. It is only when one realizes that this wrinkled dwarf of a man has the immense power of the state behind him that any notions about the banality of evil disappear. . . .

THE RIOT ACT CONSPIRACY

"Conspiracy" literally means to breathe together. In a conspiracy trial it is not necessary for the prosecution to show that the defendants ever met together or even knew each other. Their concurrence on a course of action may be inferred from overt acts which (although they may be legal in themselves—such as speaking at a rally) show that the defendants shared similar intent, that they "breathed the same air."

The federal "anti-riot" act makes it a crime punishable by five years imprisonment and a $10,000 fine for anyone to travel from one state to another, write a letter, send a telegram, make a phone call or speak over radio or television with the intent to encourage any person to participate in a riot. A "riot" is defined as "any act of . . . violence by one or more persons part of an assemblage of three . . . which shall result in injury to the property of any other person." The act further provides that a "riot" can exist without any violence actually having occurred; it is only necessary that a violent act be *threatened* or that there be a clear and present danger of violence occurring.

The eight defendants are each charged with one count of violating the anti-riot law and one count of conspiring to violate it. The first criminal act is their intent to encourage a riot; on the conspiracy count, the crime is literally the intent to intend this.

The law itself is so broad as to virtually outlaw protest. In the words of defendant [Students for a Democratic Society leader] Tom Hayden, it "would make illegal almost everything that has been done in the protest movement in the past ten years, so sweeping and so devastating is it in the kinds of things it makes illegal."

PASSING ANTI-RIOT LEGISLATION

The anti-riot law was first introduced in 1967 after the Newark and Detroit rebellions, with strong backing from Southern senators, including Strom Thurmond. Unable to get the bill through Congress for over a year, supporters finally succeeded in attaching it as a rider to the 1968 civil rights open housing law (the "King Memorial Civil Rights Act"). It was the South's price for that bill's passage in the tense period immediately following Martin Luther King's assassination.

Ramsey Clark, then U.S. Attorney General—and by no means a radical or even a maverick—opposed the anti-riot bill in congressional hearings, arguing among other things that it was a violation of First Amendment rights. After the elections,

Clark warned that if the new administration used the anti-riot act against the Chicago demonstrators, "It would be a clear sign that a crackdown was on its way."

Despite the opposition of the Attorney General, the indictments against the Eight were already being prepared during the Johnson Administration. (Preparations apparently began as far back as the Democratic Convention itself; at least one of the defendants was told by undercover agents at the time that he was to be indicted along with six or seven other leaders under the anti-riot act.) Clark, however, refused to prosecute. He focused instead on police brutality, basing his actions on a Reconstruction act which makes it illegal for a law enforcement officer to deprive a suspect of his constitutional rights by administering punishment before trial. . . .

EXTRADITING BOBBY SEALE

Indictments against the eight were presented by the Grand Jury in March 1969. Originally, Judge Campbell, whose crusade led to the indictments, selected himself to try the case. This was thought to be too blatant, however, and the Conspiracy case was reassigned to the court of Julius Hoffman.

In a pretrial court session Hoffman denied 35 out of 35 defense motions, including one for discovery of wiretap evidence and one for a six-week delay in the trial while Charles Garry, chief lawyer for the Eight, recovered from a gall bladder operation in California.

Meanwhile, Bobby Seale was arrested in Berkeley, California, on charges of conspiring to commit murder in Connecticut. While Seale was fighting extradition to the East Coast, federal marshals spirited him away without informing either his family or lawyers of his whereabouts. A San Francisco federal judge ordered that Seale be returned, but U.S. marshals stalled, claiming not to know where he was, and finally announced that Seale was in Sacramento, outside the San Francisco judge's jurisdiction. After a week-long journey by car, Seale arrived in Chicago where he was incarcerated in the Cook County Jail. William Kunstler, one of the two remaining lawyers in the case, filed a general appearance in behalf of Seale so that he could visit him in jail.

TYING THE HANDS OF THE DEFENSE

The trial began on September 24, with Hoffman denying all defense motions. In federal courts, the judge has the option of interviewing prospective jurors himself to determine prejudice, rather than allowing the attorneys to do it. The judge supposedly asks questions from lists submitted by both defense and prosecution. In the Chicago Eight case, Judge Hoffman picked the jury in two hours and fifty minutes, rejecting all the questions submitted by the defense and making only such inquiries as "Can you be fair?" Hoffman even refused to ask prospective jurors whether they had read about the case that day in the paper.

After the lawyers completed their opening statements, Seale attempted to make his own statement to the jury. Judge Hoffman ordered Seale to sit down, ruling—as he continued to rule throughout the first stage of the trial—that Seale was represented by Kunstler because of the appearance that Kunstler had filed earlier. Seale denied that he had ever chosen Kunstler as his lawyer in the case and claimed he could only be adequately represented by Charles Garry. He had fired Kunstler, as he had the right to do, before the beginning of the trial— before any evidence was introduced or witnesses sworn in. Since Garry was not there, he planned to represent himself. For this, Seale was cited for contempt, the first of 16 counts.

Next, Hoffman jailed two of the four young attorneys who had been retained to do pretrial work on the case. Never having planned to defend the Eight in court, they had formally withdrawn from the case by telegram instead of flying thousands of miles to withdraw in person. Hoffman's response— citing the four for contempt, ordering their arrest, and briefly placing two in jail—led to lawyers' demonstrations around the country. "It is an outrage unparalleled in American judicial history," declared Professor Alan Dershowitz of the Harvard Law School.

So began the fair trial of the Conspiracy Eight. The atmosphere which Hoffman established at the outset of the trial was reinforced by the heavy security maintained in the Federal Building and in the courtroom itself. . . .

THE EVIDENCE

Testimony about the eight defendants has been sparse. The government has little evidence of criminal acts committed by anyone during the demonstrations and none whatsoever that would point to an agreement among these defendants to come to Chicago.

Government evidence falls into two categories. One is recorded speeches and interviews of the defendants urging people to come to Chicago. Generally these turn out to be mild statements which could have been made by any peace movement organizer about any demonstration.

The other type of evidence is the testimony of undercover policemen who followed the defendants during the Chicago Convention. Introduced in an attempt to show that the defendants committed acts in Chicago to further their conspiracy, this testimony comes out wildly jumbled and filled with contradictions, reflecting more about the fantasies of the police than about the actions of the demonstrators. [Defendant] Jerry Rubin, for example, was credited with making a speech in Lincoln Park (on a day when he was home sick) befitting Napoleon at Moscow: "Hold the park at all costs. Arm yourselves and defeat the pigs. If the pigs take the park all is lost. Tomorrow is the day we march down to disrupt the convention. We must be prepared to sacrifice our lives. Ask my marshals for further instructions."

"How did the crowd react?" the agent was primed by the prosecution.

"With wild cheering."

"Were any swear words used?"

"Objection," Kunstler was on his feet. "The type of language the defendant allegedly used is not in question, it is not relevant, it is not what he is being tried for."

"Overruled, it is relevant," said Hoffman. The defendants are being tried for their language, their beliefs, their life-style.

"He used swear words every other sentence. Get the blankety-blank pigs, beat the blankety-blank out of them."

"What did he say afterwards?"

"He talked to Rennie Davis and said 'I'll meet you at the command post at 4:30.'"

Listening to this in his courtroom seat, the 31-year-old co-founder of the Youth International Party [Yippies] was overcome with laughter, as were most of the spectators. But the jury sat, stoney-faced, staring at Rubin. . . .

Perspective will be a large part of how they [the jury] evaluate the evidence. For instance, the government spent three days and ten witnesses trying to prove that John Froines, a hitherto unknown chemistry professor from Eugene, Oregon, made a stink bomb. For this, he may go to jail for ten years. The prosecution maintains that Froines bought butyric acid (which smells like vomit) from a Chicago chemical supply house and gave it to two women who were subsequently arrested for stink bombing the "Charade-a-go-go" nightclub in the Palmer House. In one woman's purse the police found letters to [student activist leader] Tom Hayden (from Hanoi, incidentally). The other woman had once been seen talking to Froines. The government's assumption, though never proven, is that "mad scientist" Froines and "wild communist" Hayden somehow put the women up to the act in order to further their conspiracy to create a riot.

The government has also zeroed in on Tom Hayden, citing the fact that he disguised himself after being arrested twice at the beginning of the convention week. Very conspiratorial. Hayden sleeps through much of the trial, spending the rest of his time speaking and organizing the defense. He sees the trial as part of a crackdown on revolutionary dissent being carried out by the Nixon Administration. He feels that Nixon is trying to shock and horrify the liberals, especially those in the law profession, by railroading this case through and showing them that they can do nothing about it. He believes that Nixon would like to have the liberals running scared, so that he could then isolate and smash the left.

There has been almost no evidence against Rennie Davis or Dave Dellinger. Identified with the National Mobilization Committee [Mobe] during the convention, and with the New Mobe now, the two seemed in the early part of the trial more interested in mounting a successful Mobilization than concerned about the trial. Davis thinks the trial is being held in order to crush the anti-war movement, thereby freeing Nixon to reduce ground operations in Viet-Nam while increasing air attacks and firebombings, in an attempt to cut down U.S. casualties and "win" the war by a massive slaughter of the people of Viet-Nam. . . .

BOBBY SEALE AS A FOCAL POINT

From the original announcement of the indictments, the central figure in the trial has been Black Panther Party Chairman Bobby Seale. His presence in the trial would have drawn attention in any case, but the fact that he was deprived of his right to defend himself in the absence of his lawyer, Charles Garry, made Seale the focal point of the courtroom.

Throughout the trial Seale acted without respect for the court, but with great dignity. His voice came through clear and strong, and while he was speaking, even the judge dared not interrupt. Seale looked thin, his face drawn and tired, but there was still fire in his eyes and voice. He got up to speak only at the appropriate times, at the beginning of each morning's session and at the proper time to cross-examine a witness who had testified against him. Although the press referred to his actions as "violent outbursts," all he usually did was to demand his constitutional right to act in his own defense. Only when his rights were denied did he lash out, calling the judge a "fascist," "racist," or "pig."

As tension over Seale's demands mounted (both inside and outside the courtroom), U.S. Attorney Schultz moved for a confrontation, reporting falsely to the judge that the Panther leader had addressed the spectators before the morning session, urging them to attack the marshals. . . .

[After the confrontation] Seale was bound and gagged, but not silenced. As the defendants looked on in horror, Seale's restraints were increased, and the straps tightened. [David] Dellinger threw himself in front of the marshals; Seale yelled out, "Don't kick me in the balls, motherfucker." Angry words were shouted from the lawyers to Judge Hoffman, as Rennie Davis spoke to the jury and Tom Hayden addressed the spectators, pleading for an end to the inhuman treatment of Seale.

Kunstler, speaking in obvious anguish, addressed the judge: "When are we going to stop the medieval torture chamber that is going on in this court? . . . I feel so utterly ashamed to be an American lawyer at this time."

The judge's reply: "You *should* feel ashamed of your conduct in this case, sir."

Despite the restraints, Seale continued to demand, in a muffled but quite understandable voice, his right to cross-examine witnesses and conduct his own defense. . . .

Judge Hoffman Retaliates

The gags and chains, which had been introduced on a Thursday, were removed without explanation on the following Monday. The press hinted that the move had resulted from "negotiations" with the defense; in fact, no such bargaining had taken place. The government simply realized that the sight of the black man bound and gagged was evoking too much sympathy from the jury and too much outrage on the part of world opinion.

With the gag off, Seale continued to insist upon his right to represent himself. When a prosecution witness, a County Sheriff's deputy from California, testified that he had followed Seale to the airport the day he had gone to Chicago, Kunstler refused to cross-examine, maintaining that the witness had testified only against Seale, and that he did not represent the Panther leader.

Seale then got up, walked to the lectern and began shooting questions at the deputy: "Why did you follow me?" "Have you ever participated in raids on Black Panther Party offices or on party member's homes?" "Have you ever killed a member of the Black Panther Party?" He got no answers.

Furious, Hoffman ordered Seale to sit down, then recessed the court an hour and a half early. The judge was so upset that he neglected to excuse the jury until reminded to do so by Foran.

When court resumed, Hoffman announced that he was finding Seale guilty of contempt. For the next hour and a half he read from the court record to chronicle his findings. In love with his voice and acting ability, he gave tasteless flourishes to his reading of the exchanges between himself and Seale. As the spectators sat numb, Hoffman declared Seale guilty of 16 instances of contempt, sentenced him to three months on each count, and declared his case a mistrial. Seale, still stunned, demanded an immediate trial. As he was led away, he continued to shout: "I still want an immediate trial. You can't call it a mistrial." Then a few seconds of silence. "I'm put in jail for four years for nothing!" Then, quieter, "I want my coat." The spectators ignored the marshals and stood up for him, shouting "Power to the People" and "Free Bobby."

On a purely personal level the sentence against Seale was a petty act of vengeance by a two-bit tyrant judge. Bested in his own court—his tiny kingdom—by a man who is mentally, morally, and physically superior to him, Julius Hoffman punished Seale out of spite.

But Hoffman's move had political significance as well. The government, believing that the black liberation movement can be crushed by eliminating its leaders, wants to see Seale (if not electrocuted in Connecticut) behind bars for the rest of his life; and they don't care what pretense they use to get him there.

Refusal to Do Military Service Is Not a Civil Right

HENRY PACHTER

Some of the most heated debate over the Vietnam War revolved around the issue of draft dodging. Draft dodging was an act of nonviolent protest that was intended to show the federal government that an individual could not be coerced into fighting a war, even if the consequences involved mandatory prison time. Draft dodgers typically burned their draft cards, refused to report to active duty when called into service, or left the United States for Canada, a country that did not have any established extradition treaties with the United States. Critics of the antiwar movement viewed draft dodging as an act of cowardice tantamount to treason.

Henry Pachter is a political essayist and socialist. He was a frequent contributor to liberal magazines such as *Dissent* during the 1960s, and he has written several essays on the application of socialist theory in modern democratic countries. In the following article, written in 1966, Pachter asserts that individuals may have moral arguments against war, but that they do not have a constitutional right to refuse to participate in one unless a legal battle in the federal court system provides them with that right.

In discussions about people who wish to refuse the draft, one frequently hears the argument: "These demonstrators are chicken." Such attempts to disqualify the protest as not idealistically motivated seem to me utterly irrelevant. Of course the person who objects to being drafted does so because he values his life more than any values he is being called on to de-

Henry Pachter, "Uses and Abuses of Civil Disobedience," *Dissent*, vol. 13, May/June 1966, pp. 314–17. Copyright © 1966 by Dissent Publishing Corporation. Reproduced by permission.

fend. He does not claim to be a hero, but to follow reason. And it takes a lot of courage to follow reason when everybody expects you to act like a hero. The reasonable man says: "Look here, I admit I am a coward to the extent that I will not be stampeded into saying I am a hero just to prove that I am no coward." The draft objectors need not claim that their protest is disinterested; on the contrary, they should admit that their motives are solidly materialistic and selfish—either that going to war would inconvenience them, maybe even expose them to danger, or that they cannot bear to inflict death on others. This, it seems to me, is the legitimate motive of every one who uses all the legal loopholes to avoid the draft.

Using Loopholes in the Law

Among the loopholes available to draftees, there is one which some wish they had thought of earlier: religious objection to military service. Some people now discover that they have hated war all the time, and they seek exemption on the ground of their pacifist philosophy. The law prescribes that you can claim this exemption only if you have previously given proof of your earnestness. You must be a bona fide member of a religious group that rejects military service and you must have submitted to the discipline of such a group, have undertaken some rigorous and demanding task that tested your earnestness.

At present this loophole seems to me both too narrow and too wide. It permits people to claim religious exemption on the sole ground of membership, though they may never have shown any real concern for the works of peace; but it also excludes people who have made enormous sacrifices for peace, yet whose cause happens not to qualify.

Critiquing the Use of Religion to Dodge the Draft

Yet another group of draftees consists of new converts; their abhorrence of warlike pursuits emerged only when the board of their neighbors was breathing down their necks. Some among them may actually be described as pacifist; but if they had not felt strongly enough to engage in pacifist activities earlier, they can hardly claim to be legally excused from serving. No matter how strongly they now feel that war is immoral, I think it immoral to defer the disclosure of such feelings until it helps in securing deferment. If their repugnance of service is really as strong as they now say it is, let them engage in civil disobedience and face a court; let them risk going to jail as proof of their sincerity.

ALTERNATIVES FOR PACIFISTS

The usual answer is: Why send them to jail? Would it not be more reasonable to let them do some useful work? Could they not volunteer for medical service, research, Peace Corps? By all means, provided the work entails risk, danger and discomfort comparable to combat conditions yet is not connected with the war effort. I think these two conditions follow from

A group of hippies protests the draft. The issue of draft dodging sparked heated debates during the Vietnam War.

the assumption that a principle is involved for these persons. They want to show that their refusal to serve is not motivated by fear or convenience. They also wish to establish that they are against war as such. Otherwise they would merely be asking *personally* to be left out of the dirty part of it.

There is another group of objectors who claim that they may not be strictly pacifist and would defend their country in case of attack, but who fail to see the present war in such a light. They feel that the present war is imperialist or colonialist, that it is conducted in a fashion unbecoming to a great democracy, and that it may bring us close to atomic extinction. In other words, these objectors feel that it is their duty to reserve judgment in each individual case and, if they find their government in the wrong, to agitate against the war.

If this is really their feeling, then the worst thing they could do would be to remain silent. To ask for a legal exemption from the draft on the ground that you ought to act as a defeatist, while simultaneously asking for admittance to some labor camp or medical chore is immoral. It amounts to freeing another man for military service and to asking the Government to allow some people legally to opt out of the war. They should be allowed to save their personal "conscience," but if their objection were truly political, they would seek a political, not a legal recourse.

CIVIL DISOBEDIENCE IS THE ONLY POLITICAL OPTION

The only way to opt out politically is to disobey: that is, to defy the majority and the law. There is only one way to proclaim that a particular war is wrong, and that is by declaring that the government is wrong, that its laws are wrong and that its system is wrong. I know of no historical example where a government protected its enemies from the consequences of its policies. . . .

The determination of civil disobedience, or the hardship one is ready to take upon oneself, obviously will vary with the strength of one's feelings about war in general and with one's evaluation of this particular war. You may encourage mild draft-dodging. You may engage in desperate acts of sabotage and disobedience. But one thing you cannot do: you cannot practice civil disobedience with the aid of the law; you cannot be a rebel with the consent of the Government.

The right to advocate a different course of policy for the Government, even the right to advocate resistance, is guaranteed by the Constitution. But there is no civil right to disobey a law of which one disapproves. One fights for specific civil rights, such as the right to vote, to live where one pleases etc., but disobedience itself is no civil right, even if the law in question is immoral. The fight against an immoral law may require revolutionary action, civil disobedience or even violence; but the right to start such a fight is a moral, not a legal right. If the right to revolution were a civil right, the word revolution would have no meaning. Likewise, unless he abandons citizenship, no one has a right to opt out of a national enterprise, and still less can the Government be forced—other than by revolution—to guarantee, let alone to organize such opting-out.

The Government does not recognize a citizen's right to undo its policies or to obstruct the implementation of its laws other than by testing their validity in court or by changing them through prescribed constitutional procedures. In certain cases an officer of the Government may give a citizen the order to commit deeds that are repugnant to his moral instincts or to recognized standards of human conduct. Then the citizen must fight back, and often he may have to defend himself before a military court. Resistance against the draft is often advocated on the ground that the citizen *may* get into such a conflict once he has been enrolled in the Army. Or the right to refuse the draft may be claimed on the ground that those who are not actually engaged in immoral actions may release others to commit them. Finally, the right to opt out may be claimed on the ground that war itself is the crime that is repugnant to individual conscience.

To all these arguments I answer that dissent from the present war or refusal to do any military service can only be conceived as an act of resistance, disobedience, defiance or defection. Such acts create a revolutionary right, but they cannot be claimed under any notion of civil or constitutional rights within the system that is at war. Whether an individual citizen will avail himself of this moral right to revolution will depend on the strength of his conviction, on the nature of the system and of the war, on the kind of command he is objecting to, maybe even on the nature of the enemy and, last not least, on the strength of the majority and the possibility that it may be right.

The FBI's Covert Operations Against Protesters

ANITA LOUISE MCCORMICK

In 1956 the Federal Bureau of Investigation (FBI) established the Counterintelligence Program (COINTELPRO) to investigate the activities of known and suspected Communists within the United States. FBI agents, posing as sympathetic supporters, attended Communist Party meetings to collect information that could be used to tarnish the reputations of people categorized as un-American. Many individuals who attended these meetings found themselves the subject of political persecution. These Communist sympathizers often lost their jobs and were blacklisted from employment elsewhere. During the 1960s, the FBI turned COINTELPRO against many of the liberal groups protesting for civil rights and against the Vietnam War. These groups included Students for a Democratic Society (SDS), the Student Nonviolent Coordinating Committee (SNCC), and the Black Panther Party. FBI agents posing as liberal sympathizers documented as much information on as many individual protesters as they could find and submitted their findings to prosecutors within the Justice Department.

In the following selection, author Anita Louise McCormick provides an overview of COINTELPRO and discusses strategies used by student activists to combat the FBI's covert efforts into their activities. McCormick is a freelance writer who publishes historical books for young adults. Her most popular series is In American History, which includes titles such as *The Vietnam Antiwar Movement, Native Americans and the Reservation, The Industrial Revolution, Space Exploration,* and *The Pony Express.*

A s opposition to the Vietnam War grew, government agencies were becoming increasingly concerned. The Federal Bureau of Investigation (FBI), Central Intelligence Agency (CIA), Department of Justice [DOJ], and other government agencies were used in covert (secret) and sometimes illegal attacks against antiwar leaders.

THE NEW LEFT COUNTERINTELLIGENCE PROGRAM

On October 28, 1968, the FBI launched a secret program known as the New Left COINTELPRO (Counterintelligence Program). It targeted antiwar groups the FBI felt were working to bring down or disrupt the United States government. The goal of COINTELPRO was to "expose, disrupt, misdirect, discredit or otherwise neutralize" organizations that opposed United States government policies on the war in Vietnam.

FBI agents in COINTELPRO targeted every antiwar group and activist the government saw as a threat. As the first step of the investigation, COINTELPRO had FBI agents prepare reports about antiwar groups. Topics included how they were organized, who financed them, how many members they had, if they were under Communist influence, their political activities, religious beliefs, and whether they were likely to commit acts of violence. COINTELPRO was especially interested in monitoring antiwar groups that believed in destroying government buildings or using violence to achieve their goals.

THE WEATHERMEN

One such organization was the Weathermen, an ultraradical group believed to have about four hundred members. In 1968, the Weathermen launched a campaign in Chicago called "Days of Rage." During the campaign, two hundred Weathermen and one hundred Weatherwomen marched down streets wearing helmets and carrying metal pipes. They broke windows and vandalized businesses. By the end of the demonstration, 290 of the demonstrators had been arrested.

The Weathermen were never able to gain enough members to hold large demonstrations. Eventually, many of the group's leaders became terrorists who were constantly on the run from the police. By the time the Vietnam War was over, the Weathermen had bombed nineteen induction centers, recruiting offices, and other government buildings across the nation.

But COINTELPRO also kept a close eye on peaceful antiwar demonstrations, photographing and trying to identify as many of the protesters as possible. When protesters were arrested, their names were immediately sent to FBI offices in their region.

THE DISTRIBUTION OF PROPAGANDA

Part of COINTELPRO's activities involved FBI agents printing and distributing materials that were intended to confuse and discourage antiwar protesters. COINTELPRO altered the dates of demonstrations and gave incorrect information on when buses would arrive to take people to demonstrations in distant cities, in an effort to prevent people from attending.

As part of the campaign against the antiwar movement, the FBI sent anonymous letters to the parents of students involved in protest activities. Often, the agent who wrote the letter pretended to be either a concerned friend who was interested in the student's welfare or the parent of a fellow student. One such letter read:

Dear Mr. and Mrs. Jones,

I feel you should be advised that your son, who is a fellow student . . . has recently become engrossed in activities which are not only detrimental to our country, our efforts in Vietnam and our common desire for justice, but are extremely detrimental to himself. Many of the people your son has been associated with are confirmed "Left Wingers" and some brazenly advocate communist ideology. While you may be somewhat unconcerned about your son's activities, I am sure you are cognizant of the fact that he is establishing for himself a stigma which soon he may not be able to erase. Although I would like to sign my name to this letter I do consider your son a friend of mine and would hate to lose his friendship. . . .

Agents in COINTELPRO used letters to serve other goals, as well. Using fictitious names, they wrote to superintendents of schools where young people who had been involved in antiwar activities sought to get teaching jobs. The letters discouraged the school districts from hiring anyone who was such "a radical and trouble-maker."

ACTIVISTS REVEAL COINTELPRO ACTIVITIES TO CONGRESS

On March 8, 1971, a group of antiwar activists calling itself the Citizen's Commission to Investigate the FBI, broke into the FBI offices in Media, Pennsylvania, and found thousands of classified documents about COINTELPRO's activities. Copies of these documents were sent to congressmen who had spoken out against the Vietnam War, journalists, and newspapers such as *The Washington Post* and *The New York Times*.

Each mailing included a letter that explained why the group had broken into the FBI building. The letter said:

> We have taken this action because we believe that democracy can survive only in an order of justice, of an open society and public trust, because we believe that citizens have the right to scrutinize and control their own government and because we believe that the FBI has betrayed its democratic trust.

In 1973, FBI Director Clarence M. Kelly defended COINTELPRO by declaring that the intent of the program was to "prevent dangerous acts against individuals, organizations and institutions—public and private—across the United States." He went on to say that the two thousand FBI employees in these programs "had acted in good faith and within the bounds of what was expected of them by the president, the attorney general, Congress, and, I believe, a majority of the American people."

Still, many people felt that the FBI had gone too far in its investigations and harassment of antiwar activists.

LEFTIST INVESTIGATIONS HAVE PRESIDENTIAL CONSENT

During the Vietnam War, President Johnson ordered the CIA to start a program called Operation Chaos to investigate antiwar activists. CIA agents in this program tapped phones, opened mail, and broke into the homes of people who were known to be active in the antiwar movement.

Historian Lawrence S. Wittner wrote, "The C.I.A. was soon maintaining files on 300,000 Americans, the F.B.I. on over a million. More military intelligence agents spied on American peace protesters than were employed in any other operation throughout the world." But despite all the government's efforts to connect antiwar leaders with outside Communist influences, they were not able to find one case in which the North Vietnamese government sent money or gave orders to American antiwar groups.

THE POWER OF AMERICAN MEDIA OVER PUBLIC OPINION

The Hanoi [North Vietnamese] government, however, realized the power the American media had over public opinion. Truong Nhu Tang, the North Vietnamese minister of justice, said that the American media "is easily open to suggestion and false information given by Communist agents. The [American] society is completely hypnotized by the media." So the North Vietnamese looked for ways to make the American media work for their cause.

HANOI JANE SPEAKS OUT

One way the Hanoi government influenced the media was to invite well-known American writers, entertainers, journalists, clergy members, and antiwar leaders to visit North Vietnam. The North Vietnamese showed these prominent Americans the damage that had been done by the United States military and talked about their desire to find some way of achieving a lasting peace.

In 1972, American actress Jane Fonda went on one of these tours. During her visit, she posed for photos on a North Vietnamese tank, which was used to shoot down American planes. She also made several broadcasts over Radio Hanoi. During these broadcasts, she told American pilots who flew bombing missions over Vietnam that they were no better than the war criminals who had served under German dictator Adolf Hitler during World War II. She also encouraged American military personnel to disobey orders given by their commanders. These actions were very unpopular. They earned Fonda the nickname "Hanoi Jane" among those who supported America's involvement in the Vietnam War.

Martin Luther King Denounces the Vietnam War

MARTIN LUTHER KING JR.

In the early 1960s, Martin Luther King Jr. focused on ending legalized racial discrimination in the South, but after the passage of the Civil Rights Acts of 1964 and 1965, King turned his efforts to exposing human rights violations. He believed one of the greatest inequalities in American society was the disproportionate number of poor whites and African Americans drafted into the Vietnam War. Most affluent whites of draft age qualified for draft exemption based on their status as college or university students, but most of America's poor whites and minorities, lacking education or money to attend college, were vulnerable to the draft.

By 1967, King had become one of the nation's most prominent opponents of the Vietnam War. In his "Beyond Vietnam" speech, delivered at New York's Riverside Church on April 4, 1967, a year to the day before he was murdered, King called the United States the world's greatest purveyor of violence. King denounced the war as an attack on the nation's poor. He argued that America's attempt to establish democracies in Third World nations by military force was the wrong way to bring about political and global change. King also critiqued U.S. economic intervention in other nations, complaining that the United States wasted huge sums of money supporting foreign capitalist industry while ignoring both the needs of the people of these nations and the needs of the people in the United States.

Martin Luther King Jr., address to Riverside Church, New York, April 4, 1967. Copyright © 1967 by The Heirs to the Estate of Martin Luther King Jr. Reproduced by permission of the Writers House, Inc.

I come to this magnificent house of worship tonight because my conscience leaves me no other choice. I join you in this meeting because I am in deepest agreement with the aims and work of the organization which has brought us together, Clergy and Laymen Concerned About Vietnam. The recent statements of your executive committee are the sentiments of my own heart, and I found myself in full accord when I read its opening lines: "A time comes when silence is betrayal." That time has come for us in relation to Vietnam. . . .

A PASSIONATE PLEA

I come to this platform tonight to make a passionate plea to my beloved nation. This speech is not addressed to Hanoi or to the National Liberation Front. It is not addressed to China or to Russia. Nor is it an attempt to overlook the ambiguity of the total situation and the need for a collective solution to the tragedy of Vietnam. Neither is it an attempt to make North Vietnam or the National Liberation Front paragons of virtue, nor to overlook the role they must play in the successful resolution of the problem. While they both may have justifiable reasons to be suspicious of the good faith of the United States, life and history give eloquent testimony to the fact that conflicts are never resolved without trustful give and take on both sides. Tonight, however, I wish not to speak with Hanoi and the National Liberation Front, but rather to my fellow Americans.

Since I am a preacher by calling, I suppose it is not surprising that I have seven major reasons for bringing Vietnam into the field of my moral vision. There is at the outset a very obvious and almost facile connection between the war in Vietnam and the struggle I and others have been waging in America. A few years ago there was a shining moment in that struggle. It seemed as if there was a real promise of hope for the poor, both black and white, through the poverty program. There were experiments, hopes, new beginnings. Then came the buildup in Vietnam, and I watched this program broken and eviscerated as if it were some idle political plaything of a society gone mad on war. And I knew that America would never invest the necessary funds or energies in rehabilitation of its poor so long as adventures like Vietnam continued to draw men and skills and money like some demonic, destructive suction tube. So I was increasingly compelled to see the war as an enemy of the poor and to attack it as such.

VIETNAM IS A WAR AGAINST AMERICA'S POOR

Perhaps a more tragic recognition of reality took place when it became clear to me that the war was doing far more than devastating the hopes of the poor at home. It was sending their sons and their brothers and their husbands to fight and to die in extraordinarily high proportions relative to the rest of the population. We were taking the black young men who had been crippled by our society and sending them eight thousand miles away to guarantee liberties in Southeast Asia which they had not found in southwest Georgia and East Harlem. So we have been repeatedly faced with the cruel irony of watching Negro and white boys on TV screens as they kill and die together for a nation that has been unable to seat them together in the same schools. So we watch them in brutal solidarity burning the huts of a poor village, but we realize that they would hardly live on the same block in Chicago. I could not be silent in the face of such cruel manipulation of the poor.

ATTACKING AMERICA'S USE OF VIOLENCE

My third reason moves to an even deeper level of awareness, for it grows out of my experience in the ghettos of the North over the last three years, especially the last three summers. As I have walked among the desperate, rejected, and angry young men, I have told them that Molotov cocktails and rifles would not solve their problems. I have tried to offer them my deepest compassion while maintaining my conviction that social change comes most meaningfully through nonviolent action. But they asked, and rightly so, "What about Vietnam?" They asked if our own nation wasn't using massive doses of violence to solve its problems, to bring about the changes it wanted.

Their questions hit home, and I knew that I could never again raise my voice against the violence of the oppressed in the ghettos without having first spoken clearly to the greatest purveyor of violence in the world today: my own government. For the sake of those boys, for the sake of this government, for the sake of the hundreds of thousands trembling under our violence, I cannot be silent.

For those who ask the question, "Aren't you a civil rights leader?" and thereby mean to exclude me from the movement for peace, I have this further answer. In 1957, when a group of us formed the Southern Christian Leadership Conference, we chose as our motto: "To save the soul of America." We were convinced that we could not limit our vision to certain rights for black people, but instead affirmed the conviction that America would never be free or saved from itself until the descendants of its slaves were loosed completely from the shackles they still wear. . . .

As if the weight of such a commitment to the life and health of America were not enough, another burden of responsibility was placed upon me in [1964]. And I cannot forget that the Nobel Peace Prize was also a commission, a commission to work harder than I had ever worked before for the brotherhood of man. This is a calling that takes me beyond national allegiances. . . .

America Must Recognize Vietnam's Independence

And as I ponder the madness of Vietnam and search within myself for ways to understand and respond in compassion, my mind goes constantly to the people of that peninsula. I speak now not of the soldiers of each side, not of the ideologies of the Liberation Front, not of the junta in Saigon, but simply of the people who have been living under the curse of war for almost three continuous decades now. I think of them, too, because it is clear to me that there will be no meaningful solution there until some attempt is made to know them and hear their broken cries.

They must see Americans as strange liberators. The Vietnamese people proclaimed their own independence in 1954—in 1945 rather—after a combined French and Japanese occupation and before the communist revolution in China. They were led by Ho Chi Minh. Even though they quoted the American Declaration of Independence in their own document of freedom, we refused to recognize them. Instead, we decided to support France in its reconquest of her former colony. Our government felt then that the Vietnamese people were not ready for independence, and we again fell victim to the deadly Western arrogance that has poisoned the international atmosphere for so long. With that tragic decision we rejected a revolutionary government seeking self-determination and a government that had been established not by China—for whom the Vietnamese have no great love—but by clearly indigenous forces that included some communists. For the peasants this new government meant real land reform, one of the most important needs in their lives.

For nine years following 1945 we denied the people of Vietnam the right of independence. For nine years we vigorously supported the French in their abortive effort to recolonize Vietnam. Before the end of the war we were meeting 80 percent of the French war costs. Even before the French were defeated at Dien Bien Phu, they began to despair of their reckless action, but we did not. We encouraged them with our huge financial and military supplies to continue the war even after they had lost the will. Soon we would be paying almost the full costs of this tragic attempt at recolonization.

After the French were defeated, it looked as if independence and land reform would come again through the Geneva Agreement. But instead there came the United States, determined that Ho should not unify the temporarily divided nation, and the peasants watched again as we supported one of the most vicious modern dictators, our chosen man, Premier Diem. The peasants watched and cringed as Diem ruthlessly rooted out all opposition, supported their extortionist landlords, and refused even to discuss reunification with the North.

The peasants watched as all of this was presided over by United States influence and then by increasing numbers of United States troops who came to help quell the insurgency that Diem's methods had aroused. When Diem was overthrown they may have been happy, but the long line of military dictators seemed to offer no real change, especially in terms of their need for land and peace.

Tyranny Under an American Invasion

The only change came from America as we increased our troop commitments in support of governments which were singularly corrupt, inept, and without popular support. All the while the people read our leaflets and received the regular promises of peace and democracy and land reform. Now they languish under our bombs and consider us, not their fellow Vietnamese, the real enemy. They move sadly and apathetically as we herd them off the land of their fathers into concentration camps where minimal social needs are rarely met. They know they must move on or be destroyed by our bombs.

So they go, primarily women and children and the aged. They watch as we poison their water, as we kill a million acres of their crops. They must weep as the bulldozers roar through their areas preparing to destroy the precious trees. They wander into the hospitals with at least twenty casualties from American firepower for one Vietcong-inflicted injury. So far we may have killed a million of them, mostly children. They wander into the towns and see thousands of the children, homeless, without clothes, running in packs on the streets like animals. They see the children degraded by our soldiers as they beg for food. They see the children selling their sisters to our soldiers, soliciting for their mothers.

What do the peasants think as we ally ourselves with the landlords and as we refuse to put any action into our many words concerning land reform? What do they think as we test out our latest weapons on them, just as the Germans tested out new medicine and new tortures in the concentration camps of Europe? Where are the roots of the independent Vietnam we claim to be building? Is it among these voiceless ones?

We have destroyed their two most cherished institutions: the family and the village. We have destroyed their land and their crops. We have cooperated in the crushing of the nation's only noncommunist revolutionary political force, the unified Buddhist Church. We have supported the enemies of the peasants of Saigon. We have corrupted their women and children and killed their men.

Now there is little left to build on, save bitterness. . . .

DECEIVING AMERICAN TROOPS

At this point I should make it clear that while I have tried in these last few minutes to give a voice to the voiceless in Vietnam and to understand the arguments of those who are called "enemy," I am as deeply concerned about our own troops there as anything else. For it occurs to me that what we are submitting them to in Vietnam is not simply the brutalizing process that goes on in any war where armies face each other and seek to destroy. We are adding cynicism to the process of death, for they must know after a short period there that none of the things we claim to be fighting for are really involved. Before long they must know that their government has sent them into a struggle among Vietnamese, and the more sophisticated surely realize that we are on the side of the wealthy, and the secure, while we create a hell for the poor.

Somehow this madness must cease. We must stop now. I speak as a child of God and brother to the suffering poor of Vietnam. I speak for those whose land is being laid waste, whose homes are being destroyed, whose culture is being subverted. I speak for the poor of America who are paying the double price of smashed hopes at home, and dealt death and corruption in Vietnam. I speak as a citizen of the world, for the world as it stands aghast at the path we have taken. I speak as one who loves America, to the leaders of our own nation: The great initiative in this war is ours; the initiative to stop it must be ours.

This is the message of the great Buddhist leaders of Vietnam. Recently one of them wrote these words, and I quote:

> Each day the war goes on the hatred increases in the heart
> of the Vietnamese and in the hearts of those of humani-
> tarian instinct. The Americans are forcing even their friends
> into becoming their enemies. It is curious that the Ameri-
> cans, who calculate so carefully on the possibilities of mil-
> itary victory, do not realize that in the process they are in-
> curring deep psychological and political defeat. The image
> of America will never again be the image of revolution,
> freedom, and democracy, but the image of violence and
> militarism.

WHAT AMERICA STANDS TO LOSE

If we continue, there will be no doubt in my mind and in the
mind of the world that we have no honorable intentions in
Vietnam. If we do not stop our war against the people of Vietnam immediately, the world will be left with no other alternative than to see this as some horrible, clumsy, and deadly game
we have decided to play. The world now demands a maturity
of America that we may not be able to achieve. It demands that
we admit that we have been wrong from the beginning of our
adventure in Vietnam, that we have been detrimental to the life
of the Vietnamese people. The situation is one in which we
must be ready to turn sharply from our present ways. In order
to atone for our sins and errors in Vietnam, we should take the
initiative in bringing a halt to this tragic war.

FIVE SUGGESTIONS FOR ENDING THE WAR

I would like to suggest five concrete things that our government should do immediately to begin the long and difficult
process of extricating ourselves from this nightmarish conflict:

Number one: End all bombing in North and South Vietnam.

Number two: Declare a unilateral cease-fire in the hope that
such action will create the atmosphere for negotiation.

Three: Take immediate steps to prevent other battlegrounds
in Southeast Asia by curtailing our military buildup in Thai-

land and our interference in Laos.

Four: Realistically accept the fact that the National Liberation Front has substantial support in South Vietnam and must thereby play a role in any meaningful negotiations and any future Vietnam government.

Five: Set a date that we will remove all foreign troops from Vietnam in accordance with the 1954 Geneva Agreement.

Part of our ongoing commitment might well express itself in an offer to grant asylum to any Vietnamese who fears for his life under a new regime which included the Liberation Front. Then we must make what reparations we can for the damage we have done. We must provide the medical aid that is badly needed, making it available in this country if necessary. Meanwhile, we in the churches and synagogues have a continuing task while we urge our government to disengage itself from a disgraceful commitment. We must continue to raise our voices and our lives if our nation persists in its perverse ways in Vietnam. We must be prepared to match actions with words by seeking out every creative method of protest possible. . . .

VIETNAM AS AN INDICATOR OF DEEPER PROBLEMS

The war in Vietnam is but a symptom of a far deeper malady within the American spirit, and if we ignore this sobering reality, we will find ourselves organizing "clergy and laymen concerned" committees for the next generation. They will be concerned about Guatemala and Peru. They will be concerned about Thailand and Cambodia. They will be concerned about Mozambique and South Africa. We will be marching for these and a dozen other names and attending rallies without end unless there is a significant and profound change in American life and policy. So such thoughts take us beyond Vietnam, but not beyond our calling as sons of the living God.

In 1957 a sensitive American official overseas said that it seemed to him that our nation was on the wrong side of a world revolution. During the past ten years we have seen emerge a pattern of suppression which has now justified the presence of U.S. military advisors in Venezuela. This need to maintain social stability for our investments accounts for the counterrevolutionary action of American forces in Guatemala. It tells why American helicopters are being used against guerrillas in Cambodia and why American napalm and Green Beret forces have already been active against rebels in Peru.

It is with such activity in mind that the words of the late John F. Kennedy come back to haunt us. Five years ago he said, "Those who make peaceful revolution impossible will make violent revolution inevitable." Increasingly, by choice or by accident, this is the role our nation has taken, the role of those who make peaceful revolution impossible by refusing to give up the privileges and the pleasures that come from the immense profits of overseas investments. I am convinced that if we are to get on the right side of the world revolution, we as a nation must undergo a radical revolution of values. We must rapidly begin the shift from a thing-oriented society to a person-oriented society. When machines and computers, profit motives and property rights, are considered more important than people, the giant triplets of racism, extreme materialism, and militarism are incapable of being conquered.

CONDUCTING A REVOLUTION OF VALUES

A true revolution of values will soon cause us to question the fairness and justice of many of our past and present policies. On the one hand we are called to play the Good Samaritan on life's roadside, but that will be only an initial act. One day we must come to see that the whole Jericho Road must be transformed so that men and women will not be constantly beaten and robbed as they make their journey on life's highway. True compassion is more than flinging a coin to a beggar. It comes to see that an edifice which produces beggars needs restructuring.

A true revolution of values will soon look uneasily on the glaring contrast of poverty and wealth. With righteous indignation, it will look across the seas and see individual capitalists of the West investing huge sums of money in Asia, Africa, and South America, only to take the profits out with no concern for the social betterment of the countries, and say, "This is not just."...

A true revolution of values will lay hand on the world order and say of war, "This way of settling differences is not just." This business of burning human beings with napalm, of filling our nation's homes with orphans and widows, of injecting poisonous drugs of hate into the veins of peoples normally humane, of sending men home from dark and bloody battlefields physically handicapped and psychologically deranged, cannot be reconciled with wisdom, justice, and love. A nation that continues year after year to spend more money on military defense than on programs of social uplift is approaching spiritual death.

America, the richest and most powerful nation in the world, can well lead the way in this revolution of values. There is nothing except a tragic death wish to prevent us from reordering our priorities so that the pursuit of peace will take precedence over the pursuit of war. There is nothing to keep us from molding a recalcitrant status quo with bruised hands until we have fashioned it into a brotherhood....

It is a sad fact that because of comfort, complacency, a morbid fear of communism, and our proneness to adjust to injustice, the Western nations that initiated so much of the revolutionary spirit of the modern world have now become the arch antirevolutionaries. This has driven many to feel that only Marxism has a revolutionary spirit. Therefore, communism is a judgment against our failure to make democracy real and follow through on the revolutions that we initiated. Our only hope today lies in our ability to recapture the revolutionary spirit and go out into a sometimes hostile world declaring eternal hostility to poverty, racism, and militarism....

TIME IS RUNNING OUT FOR CHANGE
We are now faced with the fact, my friends, that tomorrow is today. We are confronted with the fierce urgency of now. In

this unfolding conundrum of life and history, there is such a thing as being too late. Procrastination is still the thief of time. Life often leaves us standing bare, naked, and dejected with a lost opportunity. The tide in the affairs of men does not remain at flood—it ebbs. We may cry out desperately for time to pause in her passage, but time is adamant to every plea and rushes on. Over the bleached bones and jumbled residues of numerous civilizations are written the pathetic words, "Too late." There is an invisible book of life that faithfully records our vigilance or our neglect. Omar Khayyam is right: "The moving finger writes, and having writ moves on."

We still have a choice today: nonviolent coexistence or violent coannihilation. We must move past indecision to action. We must find new ways to speak for peace in Vietnam and justice throughout the developing world, a world that borders on our doors. If we do not act, we shall surely be dragged down the long, dark, and shameful corridors of time reserved for those who possess power without compassion, might without morality, and strength without sight.

Now let us begin. Now let us rededicate ourselves to the long and bitter, but beautiful, struggle for a new world. This is the calling of the sons of God, and our brothers wait eagerly for our response. Shall we say the odds are too great? Shall we tell them the struggle is too hard? Will our message be that the forces of American life militate against their arrival as full men, and we send our deepest regrets? Or will there be another message—of longing, of hope, of solidarity with their yearnings, of commitment to their cause, whatever the cost? The choice is ours, and though we might prefer it otherwise, we must choose in this crucial moment of human history.

CHRONOLOGY

1960

February 1: Four African American college students, Izell Blair, David Richmond, Franklin McCain, and Joseph Mc-Neil, are refused service by a Woolworth's waitress at a "whites only" lunch counter in Greensboro, North Carolina.

May 1: The Soviet Union shoots down a U.S. U-2 spy plane piloted by Air Force colonel Francis Gary Powers.

May 9: The federal Food and Drug Administration approves a new drug, Enovid, for use as an oral contraceptive by women.

May 10: The nuclear-powered submarine USS *Triton* completes the first totally submerged circumnavigation of the world, having followed the route of Ferdinand Magellan for thirty-six thousand miles during eighty-four days beneath the surface.

July 13: Democrats nominate John F. Kennedy for president and Lyndon B. Johnson for vice president.

July 28: Republicans nominate Richard M. Nixon for president and Henry Cabot Lodge for vice president.

September 26: The first televised presidential debate, between Kennedy and Nixon, airs to a national audience.

November 8: Kennedy and Johnson win the election.

December 20: Communist Vietnamese leader Ho Chi Minh organizes South Vietnamese Communists into the National Liberation Front (NLF) army in an attempt to overthrow the U.S.-backed Ngo Dinh Diem regime in South Vietnam.

1961

January 3: The United States breaks off diplomatic relations with Cuba because of its establishment of a Communist government.

January 20: John F. Kennedy is inaugurated as president. His inaugural address provides the famous quote, "Ask not what your country can do for you, ask what you can do for your country."

April 12: Soviet cosmonaut Yuri Gagarin becomes the first person to orbit Earth.

April 15: Twelve hundred U.S.-sponsored, anti-Castro Cuban rebels invade the Bay of Pigs. Most of the invaders are killed or captured.

May 4: The Student Nonviolent Coordinating Committee (SNCC) sponsors Freedom Rides in an attempt to desegregate interstate bus transit across the southern states.

May 5: Astronaut Alan Shepard becomes the first American to fly in a suborbital space flight.

May 14: Freedom Riders are attacked by a mob in Selma, Alabama.

August 13: East Germany erects the Berlin wall in an attempt to stop the flood of refugees escaping to democratic West Berlin. The wall closes the East–West Berlin border.

October 29: The Soviet Union detonates fifty-megaton hydrogen bomb, the largest man-made explosion in history.

December 11: President Kennedy sends four hundred American military advisers to South Vietnam to help train a South Vietnamese army.

1962

January 24: Music producer Brian Epstein signs a management contract with the Beatles.

February 9: The U.S. Army establishes the Military Assistance Command for Vietnam (MACV).

February 20: John Glenn becomes the first American to orbit Earth, in the Mercury spacecraft module *Friendship* 7.

April 16: Television news reporter Walter Cronkite begins anchoring the *CBS Evening News*, becoming the voice of America.

April 20: Local bus company, the New Orleans Citizens Company, gives free one-way ride to blacks who will leave the South and move into northern cities.

May 6: The first nuclear warhead is fired from the USS *Ethan Allen*, a Polaris-class nuclear submarine.

May 9: The first laser beam is successfully bounced off the Moon.

May 23: Astronaut Scott Carpenter orbits Earth three times in the Mercury spacecraft module *Aurora 7*.

July 10: Martin Luther King Jr. is arrested during a civil rights demonstration in Albany, Georgia.

July 17: The U.S. Senate rejects a potential Medicare bill for the elderly.

July 21: One hundred sixty civil right activists are jailed after a civil rights protest in Albany, Georgia.

August 6: Actress Marilyn Monroe is found dead in her Brentwood, California, apartment in an apparent drug overdose.

August 11: The Beach Boys release their first single, "Surfin' Safari."

August 17: The Beatles replace drummer Pete Best with Ringo Starr.

September 30: James Meredith registers for classes at the University of Mississippi.

October 16: The Cuban missile crisis begins when President Kennedy becomes aware of missiles in Cuba.

October 22: President Kennedy addresses the nation, stating his intention to impose a naval blockade on Cuba to prevent Soviet ships from unloading more weapons into Cuba.

October 28: Soviet premier Nikita Khrushchev orders the withdrawal of Soviet nuclear missiles from Cuba.

December 6: President Kennedy announces the decision to abandon the Skybolt ballistic missile program, which would have allowed nuclear missiles to launch from planes moving at high speeds, on the grounds that it is currently technologically beyond U.S. engineering.

December 14: The *Mariner 2* satellite transmits photographs of Venus back to Earth.

1963

January 14: In his inaugural speech, Alabama governor George Wallace declares, "Segregation now! Segregation forever!"

January 15: The Supreme Court begins arguments on the *Gideon* case; the eventual ruling of this case guarantees court-appointed legal representation for all defendants in all cases.

February 20: White supremacists burn the SNCC voter registration headquarters and four black-owned businesses in Greenwood, Mississippi.

February 28: SNCC members Jimmy Travis, Bob Moses, and Randolph Blackwell are shot at while returning from a voter education and registration meeting in Greenwood, Mississippi.

March 27: One hundred twenty black activists are attacked by police with dogs and fire hoses as they gather in front of the Wesleyan Methodist church in Birmingham, Alabama, before marching to the courthouse to protest voter discrimination.

April 11: City officials in Birmingham obtain an injunction preventing protest activities and demonstrations in the downtown area.

April 12: Martin Luther King Jr. and Ralph D. Abernathy go to jail in Birmingham for marching in defiance of the Birmingham injunction.

May 2: Birmingham police chief "Bull" Connor arrests and jails 958 children for marching against a local injunction banning protest demonstrations.

May 3: Bull Connor orders fire hoses and police dogs turned against activists, beginning a seven-day period of violence.

May 6: Birmingham police arrest a thousand children and adults, making the total number of activists arrested twenty-five hundred for the first week of May.

May 8: Buddhist monks conduct peaceful protests against President Ngo Dinh Diem's oppression of Buddhist monks in Vietnam; Buddhist leader Thich Quang Duc threatens mass suicide as a protest if the situation does not change.

May 9: White and black leaders negotiate an end to most of the remaining laws condoning segregation in Birmingham.

May 10: The first urban riot of the 1960s occurs in Birmingham. Black rioters burn white-owned property in response to the bombing of black businesses and property.

May 12: Professor Timothy Leary of Harvard is fired from his post for continuing his work with the psychedelic drug LSD.

May 15–16: Astronaut Gordon Cooper completes twenty-two orbits of the earth, breaking the previous Soviet record of seventeen.

May 28: NAACP field secretary Medgar Evers confirms an agreement with city officials in Jackson, Mississippi, to end segregation, but the offer is later withdrawn.

June 10: Congress enacts the Equal Pay for Women Act into law.

June 11: President Kennedy delivers his "moral crisis" speech on segregation; Governor Wallace blocks the schoolhouse door of the University of Alabama in order to prevent two black students from enrolling; James Hood and Vivian Malone become the first two black students registered at the University of Alabama; Buddhist monk Thich Quang Duc sets himself on fire in Vietnam as a protest against the social oppression of Buddhists by the Diem regime.

June 12: Medgar Evers is murdered outside his home in Jackson, Mississippi, as he returns home from work.

August 28: In Washington, D.C., 250,000 people participate in the March on Washington for civil rights; Martin Luther King Jr. delivers his "I Have a Dream" speech.

September 15: The Sixteenth Street Baptist Church in Birmingham is bombed, killing four young black Sunday school students: Addie Mae Collins, 14; Denise McNair, 11; Carol Robertson, 14; and Cynthia Wesley, 11.

October 13: A performance by the Beatles at the London Palladium is shown on American television; reactions to the performance are so favorable that the media coin the phrase "Beatlemania."

November 1: A military coup in South Vietnam overthrows and assassinates President Diem and his family.

November 22: President Kennedy is assassinated in Dallas by Lee Harvey Oswald; Vice President Lyndon B. Johnson is sworn into office as the thirty-sixth president of the United States.

November 24: Dallas business owner Jack Ruby kills accused assassin Lee Harvey Oswald in the basement of the Dallas police department, a scene broadcast live on national television; President Johnson signs a national security memorandum stating that the U.S. government's goal in Vietnam is helping the Saigon government achieve a military victory over the North Vietnamese Communists.

1964

January 8: President Johnson declares that America must conquer poverty in his "Great Society" speech.

February 9: The Beatles make their U.S. television debut on *The Ed Sullivan Show.*

February 17: The U.S. Supreme Court rules that U.S. congressional districts should be roughly equal in population.

June 21: Three Mississippi civil rights workers disappear; their bodies are discovered forty-four days later.

July 2: President Johnson signs the Civil Rights Act of 1964.

July 15: Republicans nominate U.S. senator Barry Goldwater for president.

August 4: President Johnson announces the use of air strikes by the U.S. military against North Vietnam.

September 24: The Warren Commission declares that Lee Harvey Oswald acted alone in the assassination of President Kennedy.

November 3: President Johnson wins the presidential election.

December 10: Martin Luther King Jr. is awarded the Nobel Peace Prize for his work on civil rights.

1965

February 1: Martin Luther King Jr. and more than twenty-six hundred other civil rights workers are arrested in Selma, Alabama, during demonstrations against voter registration rules.

February 7: President Johnson orders bombing raids against North Vietnam.

February 21: Nation of Islam leader Malcolm X is assassinated at a voter registration rally in Harlem in New York City.

March 7: Two hundred police attack civil rights marchers outside Selma, Alabama, in an attempt to prevent marchers from reaching Birmingham. The violence is televised and the incident becomes known as "Bloody Sunday."

March 8: The first American combat troops arrive in South Vietnam. By the end of the year, 190,000 combat troops will be in Vietnam.

June 30: President Johnson signs legislation to establish the Head Start Program, creating afternoon programs for inner-city youth.

July 4: President Johnson signs the Voter Rights Act of 1965, ending the practice of using poll taxes, literacy tests, and other obstacles to prevent African Americans from voting.

July 30: President Johnson signs legislation creating the national Medicare program.

August 11–16: Blacks riot for six days in the Watts section of Los Angeles. When the riot ends, thirty-four people are dead, over a thousand people are injured, and nearly four thousand people are arrested.

October 15: Over one hundred thousand people take part in a nationwide demonstration aginst U.S. involvement in Vietnam.

December 20: The U.S. military authorizes troops to pursue enemy soldiers into Cambodia.

1966

January 24: President Johnson submits the nation's first $100 billion budget; increased costs are due to the war effort in Vietnam and the Medicare program.

March 24: The selective service establishes college deferment policies based on academic performance, replacing the previous policy based on registration and attendance.

May 16: The Student Nonviolent Coordinating Committee elects Stokely Carmichael as its chairman; Carmichael removes all white personnel from positions of power within the group.

June 30: Betty Friedan and other feminists found the National Organization for Women (NOW).

October 15: The Black Panther Party is founded in Oakland, California.

October 22: The U.S. Supreme Court decides *Miranda v. Arizona*, protecting the civil rights of those accused of crimes. These basic rights become known as Miranda rights.

1967

January 14: Twenty-five thousand hippies crowd into San Francisco's Golden Gate park to attend a "Be-In" festival that emphasizes psychedelic music, antiwar protest, drug use, and sexual freedom.

January 16: In Tuskegee, Alabama, Lucius Amerson is sworn in as the first black southern sheriff of the twentieth century.

January 27: Three Apollo astronauts, Virgil I. Grissom, Edward White II, and Roger B. Chaffee, are killed in a spacecraft fire during a simulated launch.

July 23: Racial violence erupts in Detroit; seven thousand National Guard troops aid police after a tense night of rioting.

October 2: Thurgood Marshall is sworn in as the first black U.S. Supreme Court justice.

October 21: One hundred thousand anti–Vietnam War protesters gather at the Lincoln Memorial and march to the Pentagon, but are stopped by armed military police.

1968

January 23: The USS *Pueblo* is seized by a North Korean gunboat; the eighty-three crew members are held hostage as spies.

January 31: During a temporary truce established for the Vietnamese Tet holiday, North Vietnamese troops launch one of the largest offensive attacks against South Vietnam.

March 16: U.S. soldiers kill 347 unarmed villagers, mostly women and children, in the My Lai massacre.

March 31: President Johnson declares on national television that he will not run for reelection.

April 4: Martin Luther King Jr. is assassinated by James Earl Ray.

June 4: Robert Kennedy is shot and killed by Sirhan Bishara Sirhan in the kitchen of the Ambassador Hotel in Los Angeles after winning the Democratic presidential nomination.

July 29: Pope Paul VI upholds the Catholic ban against artificial contraception.

August 8: Republicans nominate Richard M. Nixon for president.

August 28: Democrats in Chicago nominate Hubert Humphrey for president; thousands of protesters fill the streets of Chicago and engage in violence with forty-five hundred police and National Guard units.

September 7: Radical feminists protest the Miss America Pageant.

November 6: Richard Nixon is elected president.

1969

March 10: James Earl Ray pleads guilty to the murder of Martin Luther King Jr.

June 20: The Stonewall riot in New York City marks the beginning of the gay rights movement.

July 20: U.S. astronauts Neil A. Armstrong, Edwin E. Aldrin Jr., and Michael Collins are the first people to walk on the moon.

August 15: The Woodstock Music and Arts Festival begins on a small farm outside of Bethel, New York, attracting more than 250,000 participants.

September 3: North Vietnamese leader Ho Chi Minh dies.

November 15: Some 250,000 protesters rally in Washington, D.C., to protest the war in Vietnam.

December 1: The selective service initiates a lottery to select draftees for the war.

December 14: Chicago police kill Black Panther Party leader Fred Hampton.

1970
May 4: Ohio National Guard troops kill four Kent State University students during a student-led protest against Nixon's plan to launch a major offensive into Cambodia.

June 24: Recognizing the unpopularity of the war, Congress votes to repeal the Gulf of Tonkin Resolution, which gives the president the power to take any steps necessary to ensure peace in Vietnam.

FOR FURTHER RESEARCH

General Sixties History

Jules Archer, *The Incredible Sixties.* San Diego: Harcourt Brace Jovanovich, 1986.

Rick Beard and Leslie Cohen Berlowitz, eds., *Greenwich Village: Culture and Counterculture.* New Brunswick, NJ: Rutgers University Press, 1993.

Alexander Bloom, ed., *Long Time Gone: Sixties America Then and Now.* New York: Oxford University Press, 2001.

Bob Brunning, *1960s Pop.* New York: P. Bendrick Books, 1999.

David R. Farber, *The Age of Great Dreams: America in the 1960s.* New York: Hill and Wang, 1994.

———, *The Sixties: From Memory to History.* Chapel Hill: University of North Carolina Press, 1994.

Todd Gitlin, *The Sixties: Years of Hope, Days of Rage.* New York: Bantam, 1987.

Albert Goldman, *Freakshow: Misadventures in the Counterculture, 1959–1971.* New York: Cooper Square Press, 2001.

David Horowitz, ed., *Counterculture and Revolution.* New York: Random House, 1972.

Kitty Powe-Temperley, *The 60s: Mods and Hippies.* Milwaukee: Gareth Stevens, 2000.

Irwin Unger and Debbie Unger, eds., *The Times They Were a Changin': The Sixties Reader.* New York: Three Rivers Press, 1998.

Howard Zinn, *A People's History of the United States: 1492 to the Present*. New York: HarperPerennial, 1995.

The Student Movement

Stewart Burns, *Social Movements of the 1960s: Searching for Democracy*. Boston: Twayne, 1990.

Elizabeth Hoffman Cobbs, *All You Need Is Love: The Peace Corps and the Spirit of the 1960s*. Cambridge, MA: Harvard University Press, 1993.

Dave Dellinger, *More Power than We Know: The People's Movement Toward Democracy*. Garden City, NY: Anchor Press, 1975.

Abbie Hoffman, *The Best of Abbie Hoffman*. New York: Four Walls Eight Windows, 1969.

William L. O'Neill, *Coming Apart: An Informal History of America in the 1960s*. New York: Times Books, 1971.

Donald L. Simons, *I Refuse: The Memories of a Vietnam War Objector*. Trenton, NJ: Broken Rifle Press, 1992.

Athan Theoharis, ed., *A Culture of Secrecy: The Government Versus the People's Right to Know*. Lawrence: University Press of Kansas, 1998.

Howard Zinn, *SNCC: The New Abolitionists*. Boston: Beacon Press, 1964.

The Civil Rights Movement and Black Power

Stokely Carmichael, *Black Power to Pan Africanism*. New York: Random House, 1971.

Clayborne Carson, *In Struggle: The SNCC and the Black Awakening of the 1960s*. Cambridge, MA: Harvard University Press, 1995.

E. Culpepper Clark, *The Schoolhouse Door: Segregation's Last Stand at the University of Alabama*. New York: Oxford University Press, 1993.

Dana Catherine De Ruiz and Richard Laurios, *La Causa: The Migrant Farmworker's Story*. Austin, TX: Raintree Steck-Vaughn, 1993.

Jim Haskins, *I Have a Dream: The Life and Words of Dr. Martin Luther King Jr.* Brookfield, CT: Millbrook Press, 1992.

Martin Luther King Jr., *A Call to Conscience: The Landmark Speeches of Dr. Martin Luther King Jr.* Eds. Clayborne Carson and Kris Shepard. Atlanta: Intellectual Properties Management, 2001.

Malcolm X, *By Any Means Necessary: Speeches, Interviews, and a Letter, by Malcolm X.* Ed. George Breitman. New York: Pathfinder Press, 1970.

Milton Meltzer, *There Comes a Time: The Struggle for Civil Rights.* New York: Random House, 2001.

Frances E. Ruffin, *Martin Luther King Jr. and the March on Washington*. New York: Grosset and Dunlap, 2001.

Shelby Steele, *A Dream Deferred: A Second Betrayal of Black Freedom in America.* New York: HarperCollins, 1998.

Foreign Policy Issues

Elizabeth Becker, *America's Vietnam War: A Narrative History.* New York: Clarion Books, 1992.

James G. Blight, Bruce J. Allyn, and David A. Welder, *Cuba on the Brink: Castro, the Missile Crisis, and the Soviet Collapse.* New York: Pantheon Books, 1953.

William B. Breuner, *Race to the Moon: America's Duel with the Soviets.* Westport, CT: Praeger, 1993.

Noam Chomsky, *Rethinking Camelot: JFK, the Vietnam War, and U.S. Political Culture.* Boston: South End Press, 1993.

James F. Dunnigan and Albert A. Noffi, *Dirty Little Secrets of the Vietnam War.* New York: St. Martin's Press, 1999.

George C. Hernig, *LBJ and Vietnam: A Different Kind of War.* Austin: University of Texas Press, 1994.

Arnold R. Isaacs, *Vietnam Shadows: The War, Its Ghosts, and Its Legacy.* Baltimore: Johns Hopkins University Press, 1997.

James A. Nathan, *Anatomy of the Cuban Missile Crisis.* Westport, CT: Greenwood Press, 2001.

James W. Tollefson, *The Strength Not to Fight: An Oral History of Conscientious Objectors of the Vietnam War.* Boston: Little, Brown, 1993.

James E. Westheider, *Fighting on Two Fronts: African Americans and the Vietnam War.* New York: New York University Press, 1997.

The Women's Movement

Betty Friedan, *The Feminine Mystique.* New York: Random House, 1963.

———, *It Changed My Life: Writings on the Women's Movement.* New York: Random House, 1976.

Martha Kendall, *Failure Is Impossible: The History of American Women's Rights.* Minneapolis: Lerner, 2001.

Leonard Stevens, *The Case of Roe v. Wade.* New York: G.P. Putnam's Sons, 1996.

Web Sites

The Alabama Department of Archives and History, www.archives.state.al.us. The Alabama Department of Archives and History documents many of the speeches and writings of both segregationists and integrationists whose work is considered influential in the civil rights movement in Alabama.

The Best of Kennedy Assassination Web sites, http://
mcadams.posc.mu.edu/bestof.htm. This Web site offers a
variety of useful links to Web sites that cover the Kennedy
assassination in depth and the conspiracy to assassinate President Kennedy.

The Black Panther Party, www.blackpanther.org. The Black
Panther Party, founded by Huey Newton and Bobby
Seale, was an influential Black Power advocate during the
1960s. This Web site offers a historical overview of the
group as well as information regarding the lives of members who gained fame during their involvement with the
group in the late sixties.

The CWLU Herstory Project, www.cwluherstory.com. The
Chicago Women's Liberation Union Web site offers historical perspectives on the women's movement in Chicago,
as well as a link to a historical database containing important feminist papers that shaped the women's liberation
movement during the 1960s.

The Diggers Archives, www.diggers.org. The Diggers archive
provides a general history of this influential, San Francisco–
based counterculture group. The site offers a history of the
group as well as links to several key events during the middle and late sixties in the Haight-Ashbury district.

The Martin Luther King (MLK) Papers Project, www.stanford.
edu/group/King. The Martin Luther King Papers Project
is a collection of King's most famous writings and
speeches. Extensive information about his life, involvement
in civil rights, and assassination is also available.

The Official Timothy Leary Web site, www.leary.com. This
Web site offers extensive biographical information about
Leary, several hard-to-find articles regarding his early experiments with psychedelic drugs, and links to others areas of Leary's research and interests.

The Official Web site of Malcolm X, www.cmgww.com/
historic/malcolm. The official Malcolm X Web site offers

biographical information about Malcolm X, a time line of important events in his life, and an extensive collection of links to important books, speeches, and articles both by and about Malcolm X.

The Sixties Project, http://lists.village.virginia.edu/sixties. The Sixties Project offers a collection of important primary documents that were fundamental in the emergence of the student movement and the antiwar movement.

INDEX

abortion
  legalization of, 28
  women's right to choose
    and, 127–29, 133
African Americans
  America's strategy of
    discrimination against,
    103–104
  black nationalism among,
    101–103
  fear of population growth
    of, 100–101
  low wages of, 93–94
  negative stereotypes of,
    109–10
  radicals, rejection of
    liberalism by, 122–23
  self-determination by, 128
  white supremacy and,
    94–95
American Communist Party,
  34
antiwar movement, 13
  emergence of, 23–25
  government covert
    operations against, 164–67
  lack of negotiations by
    authorities in, 40–41
  see also draft dodging
Atkinson, Ti-Grace, 124

Babbs, Ken, 83, 86, 89
Baez, Joan, 43
Beatles, the, 84
Beat veterans, 83–84

Beckwith, Byron de la, 18
Big Sur, California, 66
Birmingham, Alabama, 93
birth control pill
  drawbacks of, 137–38
  impact of, 134–36
    on Catholic women,
      138–39
    on teenage pregnancy,
      139–40
    on women in the labor
      force, 139
    on women's liberation, 26
  introduction of, 136
  problems associated with,
    135, 136
  sexual freedom with,
    136–37
Bitch Manifesto (Freeman), 28
black nationalism, 101–103
Black Panther Party, 21–23
Black Power, 20–21
"blowing people's minds," 72
Brand, Steward, 88
Brandeis, Louis, 142–43
Breines, Wini, 32
Brogan, D.W., 24–25
Brown, H. Rap, 22
bus boycotts, 16

Carmichael, Stokely, 20–21,
  108
Cassady, Neal, 89
Catholics, 139
Chicago Eight Conspiracy

Hayden, Tom, 12, 153
Henry, Aaron, 18
hippie movement
  antiachievement and, 67–68
  avoidance of work and, 73
  benefits of, 73–74
  commitment to love in, 70
  drug use and, 72–73, 84
  emergence of, 13–15
  has not disappeared, 66–67
  origin of term for, 83–84
  maintaining cohesion in,
    71–72
  political movements and,
    43–44
  value of independence in,
    70–71
  value systems of, 69–70
Hoffman, Abbie, 75
  on the New Left, 79–80
Hoffman, Julius, 23, 75, 148,
  150, 151, 155–56
Hoskyns, Barney, 82
House Un-American
  Activities Committee, 38
humanist liberals, 122
human rights, 105

Jackson, Jimmy Lee, 97
Johnson, Lyndon B., 167

"keeping your cool," 71, 74
Kelly, Clarence M., 166
Kennedy, John F., 11
Kent State shootings (1970),
  24
Kerry, John, 25
Kesey, Ken, 82
King, Martin Luther, Jr., 91,
  169

activism by, 15–17
opposition to Vietnam War
  by, 170–80
Koedt, Anne, 28
Krassner, Paul, 89
Kunstler, William, 150–51,
  152, 155

labor force
  equal rights for women in,
    144–45
  increase of women in, 120
  laws protecting women in,
    141–43
legislation
  antiriot, 149–50
  history of Equal Rights
    Amendment for women
    and, 144–45
  Jim Crow laws and, 93–94
  protecting women in the
    workplace, 141–43
  see also Civil Rights Act
    (1964)
Lewis, John, 19, 20
liberalism, rejection of,
  122–23
literacy tests, 16–17, 18
Lovin' Spoonful, the, 87
LSD
  "acid tests" with, 86–89
  group experiments with,
    82–83
  music and, 84–85
  sources of, 85–86
lunch counter sit-ins, 18–19
Lynd, Staughton, 52

Mainardi, Pat, 28
Malcolm X, 21, 99

Winters, John, 19
Wittner, Lawrence S., 167
Wolfe, Tom, 87–88
women
conventional role of, 120–21
denigration of, 129–30
excluded from reproductive
rights debate, 128–29
in the labor force, 120
motherhood and, 130
protection of minimum
wages for, 143–44
protective laws for working,
141–43
relationship between men
and, 130–32
as sex objects, 128
sex provision in Civil
Rights Act and, 144
social behavior during
1950s by, 33–34
see also sexual revolution
women's liberation
movement

concerns/issues of, 25–28
feminist movement vs., 28,
124, 125
influence of civil rights
movement on, 121–22
lofty goals of, 124–26
as a quintessential
movement, 119–20
rejection of NOW by,
123–24
Woodward, C. Vann, 93

Yippies (Youth International
Party)
beliefs/characteristics of,
77–79
disruption/chaos and,
76–77
Grand Central Station
Massacre and, 80–81
hippies and, 66–67
on the Left, 79–80
theatrical tactics of, 29, 118